The Role of the Christian Family in the Modern World

Familiaris Consortio

ANNIVERSARY EDITION

The Role of the Christian Family in the Modern World

Familiaris Consortio

ANNIVERSARY EDITION

POPE JOHN PAUL II

With commentary by John and Claire Grabowski

Pauline
BOOKS & MEDIA
Boston

Library of Congress Cataloging-in-Publication Data

Catholic Church. Pope (1978-2005 : John Paul II)
[Familiaris consortio. English]
The role of the Christian family in the modern world : Familiaris Consortio / Pope John Paul II ; with commentary by John and Claire Grabowski. -- Anniversary Edition.
    pages cm
Includes bibliographical references.
ISBN 978-0-8198-6503-8 (pbk.) -- ISBN 0-8198-6503-6 (pbk.)
1. Families--Religious life. 2. Catholic Church--Doctrines. 3. Church work with families--Catholic Church. 4. Christian life--Catholic authors. I. John Paul II, Pope, 1920-2005. II. Grabowski, John S., joint writer of added commentary. III. Title.
BX2351.C29513 2015
261.8'3585--dc23

2015000077

The Scripture quotations contained in the commentary are from the *New Revised Standard Version Bible: Catholic Edition*, copyright © 1989, 1993, Division of Christian Education of the National Council of the Churches of Christ in the United States of America. Used by permission. All rights reserved.

Excerpts from *Gratissimam Sane, Evangelii Gaudium, Gaudium et Spes, Veritatis Splendor, Laborem Exercens, Mulieris Dignitatem, Humanae Vitae, Apostolicam Actuositatem, Centesimus Annus, Lumen Gentium, Evangelium Vitae, Evening of Witness: Address of His Holiness Pope Benedict XVI* , "A Big Heart Open to God," The Prayer for the Synod of the Family and The Prayer for the New Evangelization © Libreria Editrice Vaticano. All rights reserved. Used with permission.

Cover design by Rosana Usselmann

Cover photo istockphoto.com/ © digitalskillet, © Omela

Text of *Familiaris Consortio* © Libreria Editrice Vaticano Libreria Editrice Vaticana, 00120, Cittá del Vaticana. Used with permission. All rights reserved.

"P" and PAULINE are registered trademarks of the Daughters of St. Paul.

Published by Pauline Books & Media, 50 Saint Pauls Avenue, Boston, MA 02130–3491

Printed in the U.S.A.

www.pauline.org

Pauline Books & Media is the publishing house of the Daughters of St. Paul, an international congregation of women religious serving the Church with the communications media.

1 2 3 4 5 6 7 8 9   19 18 17 16 15

Contents

❧

Preface

At the Mass for the canonization of Saints John XXIII and John Paul II, Pope Francis referred to Pope John Paul II as "the Pope of the family" and noted that this was how John Paul II himself had hoped to be remembered.[*]

Why? Why would the twentieth century's most prolific pontiff—who redefined the papacy with his incredible 104 apostolic journeys to 129 countries, his eloquence in many languages, his impact on the world stage, and his charismatic personality—want to be remembered most for his service to the family?

The reason was his deep conviction of the family's importance for the life of the Church and the world. This conviction was born of his personal experience, his observation of life as an artist and philosopher, and his work as a pastor. Family is

---

[*] Pope Francis, Homily of Pope Francis for the Holy Mass and Rite of Canonization for Blesseds John XXIII and Pope John Paul II. Available at http://w2.vatican.va/content/francesco/en/homilies/2014/documents/papa-francesco_20140427_omelia-canonizzazioni.html (accessed 9/2/14).

the place where persons learn the meaning of their own humanity—where they learn to share, to care for others, to live in the communion of truth and love. And these family members are the present and future members of the wider society. "The future of humanity passes by way of the family," he would write in this apostolic exhortation (*FC* no. 86).

The same can be said for the mission of the Church. In his Incarnation, "The only-begotten Son, of one substance with the Father . . . entered into human history through the family."[*] Salvation entered the world through the family in the Incarnation, and it continues to do so in the life of the Church. The family is "the domestic church"—the Church in miniature—carrying on Christ's work as priest, prophet, and king (see nos. 49–50).

Because of its importance, the family is often "a sign of contradiction," as Simeon prophesied of the child Jesus (see Lk 2:34). Saint John Paul II knew this well. He saw firsthand the suffering of families in his native Poland under the brutal ideologies of Nazism and Communism. In his work as philosopher and bishop, he sought to help families live and experience the Church's teaching on family despite the opposition of a hostile State. He saw the Church wracked by controversy after Pope Paul VI's encyclical *Humanae Vitae*. He also saw the devastating impact in many parts of the world of

---

[*] John Paul II, *Letter to Families* (*Gratissimam Sane*) (1994), no. 2. The citation is from http://www.vatican.va/holy_father/john_paul_ii/letters/documents/hf_jp-ii_let_02021994_families_en.html (accessed 9/2/14).

the sexual revolution—a revolution fueled by oral contraception.

On his elevation to the Chair of Peter in 1978, the family was at the top of John Paul II's pastoral agenda for the Church. Less than two months later, he announced a World Synod of Bishops on the topic of "the role of the family." This synod met in the fall of 1980 and produced propositions that formed the backdrop for *Familiaris Consortio*. Many times in his papal teaching John Paul II returned to the subject of the family and the challenges it faced. He described its vital role in building a "civilization of love"* or a "culture of life."†

John Paul II did not only teach about the family, but he also worked and suffered on its behalf. In May 1981, six months before he promulgated *Familiaris Consortio*, he founded the Pontifical Council for the Family. On his way across Saint Peter's Square to announce this new dicastery, he was felled and almost killed by a would-be assassin's bullet—an attack that he took as a sign of how the powers of evil in the world oppose the family.

For the last five years, we have had the great privilege of serving together on the Pontifical Council for the Family, giving us a sense of the truly global nature of the Church's pastoral care of families. While we never had the opportunity to meet Saint John Paul II during his life, he has had a profound and lasting influence on our own family and our

---

* See *Gratissimam Sane*, nos. 13–14.

† See the 1995 Encyclical Letter *Evangelium Vitae*, no. 26.

ministry as a couple. His teaching has helped us to better understand our own vocation as spouses and parents. It has also shaped our work in teaching, preparing couples for marriage, and doing marriage ministry.

Familiaris Consortio, the most comprehensive statement of the modern Magisterium on the family to appear in the twentieth century, gives us a vision of what the Christian family can be despite the challenges it faces. In it we hear the clarity of a trained philosopher, the voice of a poet, the heart of a pastor, the faith of a theologian, and the courage of a saint still calling out to Christian families to "become what you are" (*FC* no. 17). Let us listen again to "the Pope of the Family."

Topical Outline

**Conclusion **

APOSTOLIC EXHORTATION
OF POPE JOHN PAUL II

On the Role of the Christian Family in the Modern World

Familiaris Consortio

To the Episcopate, to the Clergy, and to
the Faithful of the Whole Catholic Church

Introduction

The Church at the service of the family

1. The family in the modern world, as much as and perhaps more than any other institution, has been beset by the many profound and rapid changes that have affected society and culture. Many families are living this situation in fidelity to those values that constitute the foundation of the institution of the family. Others have become uncertain and bewildered over their role or even doubtful and almost unaware of the ultimate meaning and truth of conjugal and family life. Finally, there are others who are hindered by various situations of injustice in the realization of their fundamental rights.

Knowing that marriage and the family constitute one of the most precious of human values, the Church wishes to speak and offer her help to those who are already aware of the value of marriage and the family and seek to live it faithfully, to those who are uncertain and anxious and searching for the truth, and to those who are unjustly impeded from living freely their family lives. Supporting the first, illuminating the second, and assisting the others, the Church offers her services to every person who wonders about the destiny of marriage and the family.[1]

In a particular way the Church addresses the young, who are beginning their journey toward marriage and family life, for the purpose of presenting them with new horizons, helping them to discover the beauty and grandeur of the vocation to love and the service of life.

The Synod of 1980 in continuity with preceding synods

2. A sign of this profound interest of the Church in the family was the last Synod of Bishops, held in Rome from September 26 to October 25, 1980. This was a natural continuation of the two preceding Synods:[2] the Christian family, in fact, is the first community called to announce the Gospel to the human person during growth and to bring him or her, through a progressive education and catechesis, to full human and Christian maturity.

Furthermore, the recent Synod is logically connected in some way as well with that on the ministerial priesthood and on justice in the modern world. In fact, as an educating community, the family must help man to discern his own vocation and to accept responsibility in the search for greater justice, educating him from the beginning in interpersonal relationships, rich in justice and in love.

At the close of their assembly, the Synod Fathers presented me with a long list of proposals in which they had gathered the fruits of their reflections, which had matured over intense days of work, and they asked me unanimously to be a spokesman before humanity of the Church's lively care for the family and to give suitable indications for renewed pastoral effort in this fundamental sector of the life of man and of the Church.

As I fulfill that mission with this Exhortation, thus actuating in a particular matter the apostolic ministry with which I am entrusted, I wish to thank all the members of the Synod for the very valuable contribution of teaching and experience that they made especially through the *Propositiones*, the text of which I am entrusting to the Pontifical Council for the Family with instructions to study it so as to bring out every aspect of its rich content.

The precious value of marriage and of the family

3. Illuminated by the faith that gives her an understanding of all the truth concerning the great value of marriage and the family and their deepest meaning, the Church once again feels the pressing need to proclaim the Gospel, that is the "good news," to all people without exception, in particular to all those who are called to marriage and are preparing for it, to all married couples and parents in the world.

The Church is deeply convinced that only by the acceptance of the Gospel are the hopes that man legitimately places in marriage and in the family capable of being fulfilled.

Willed by God in the very act of creation,[3] marriage and the family are interiorly ordained to fulfillment in Christ[4] and have need of his graces in order to be healed from the wounds of sin[5] and restored to their "beginning,"[6] that is, to full understanding and the full realization of God's plan.

At a moment of history in which the family is the object of numerous forces that seek to destroy it or in some way to deform it, and aware that the well-being of society and her own good are intimately tied to the good of the family,[7] the Church perceives in a more urgent and compelling way her mission of proclaiming to all people the plan of God for marriage and the family, ensuring their full vitality and human and Christian development, and thus contributing to the renewal of society and of the People of God.

Ponder

Marriage and the family are perennial concerns of the Church. From its beginning Christians have seen the family as vital to the Church and its mission in the world. In the rapidly evolving culture of the modern world, the family has been subjected to jarring changes and new challenges. This observation of Saint John Paul II was apt in his day. The Industrial Revolution moved economic production out of the home. The sexual revolution battered the family and the Church. The growth of communication technology made the world seem smaller.

The changes and challenges facing the family are even more pronounced in our own day. Now the very definitions of marriage and the family are under dispute. The family is threatened by a pervasive individualism and subjectivism. As Pope Francis has observed: "The family is experiencing a profound cultural crisis, as are all communities and social bonds. . . . Marriage now tends to be viewed as a form of mere emotional satisfaction that can be constructed in any way or modified at will. But the indispensable contribution of marriage to society transcends the feelings and momentary needs of the couple."[*] For many people these realities mean whatever those entering into them

---

[*] Pope Francis, Apostolic Exhortation *Evangelii Gaudium* (2013), no. 66. The citation is from http://w2.vatican.va/content/francesco/en/apost_exhortations/documents/papa-francesco_esortazione-ap_20131124_evangelii-gaudium.html (accessed 9/8/14).

want them to mean. They are simply private arrangements ordered to the happiness of individuals.

In offering this teaching over thirty years ago Saint John Paul II emphasized that the Church is at the service of the family. The Church serves the family by underscoring its great value to the human community as well as its preciousness in the eyes of its Creator. The Church does this in its own unique way by allowing the light of its faith to illuminate the family's nature and purpose. The full truth about the family emerges only in the light of God's eternal plan: "Willed by God in the very act of creation, marriage and the family are interiorly ordered to fulfillment in Christ and have need of his graces in order to be healed from the wounds of sin and restored to their 'beginning'" (*FC* no. 3).

This document was written, and the Synod that preceded it took place, while John Paul II was delivering his series of weekly general audiences, now known as the theology of the body. In them he reflected on the human person in light of the basic triptych of salvation history: creation, the fall, redemption in Christ. The aim of these reflections was to highlight the basic purpose and vocation of the human being: love. God created the person, the body in its masculinity and femininity, marriage, and religious celibacy in order to give and receive love—what the Second Vatican Council called "the sincere gift of self."* This rich catechesis forms the backdrop for many of the ideas presented in this apostolic exhortation.

---

* See *Pastoral Constitution on the Church in the Modern World* (*Gaudium et Spes*) (1995), no. 24.

1. What changes in your lifetime (whether social, economic, or technological) have impacted families in the world around you? How have these affected your own family? How have you seen the Church respond to these changes?

2. Have you witnessed the individualism and subjectivism that Pope Francis warns against in regard to the family? What happens when marriage is understood as a private arrangement ordered only to the happiness of those who enter it? What are some things that we can do to protect young people from being infected by these poisonous attitudes?

3. When you think about the family in light of God's eternal plan for the world, how does that change your perspective on your own family? Can you think of instances in the Bible where specific families played an integral role in bringing about God's plan for his people?

4. How have you experienced God's care for your family both as a child and as an adult? Have you experienced the Church's vision of family as an encouragement in your own family's life? How?

Pray

Reflect on the words of Saint Paul in his prayer to the Ephesians (3:14–21).

> For this reason I kneel before the Father, from whom every family in heaven and on earth is named, that he

may grant you in accord with the riches of his glory to be strengthened with power through his Spirit in the inner self, and that Christ may dwell in your hearts through faith; that you, rooted and grounded in love, may have strength to comprehend with all the holy ones what is the breadth and length and height and depth, and to know the love of Christ that surpasses knowledge, so that you may be filled with all the fullness of God. Now to him who is able to accomplish far more than all we ask or imagine, by the power at work within us, to him be glory in the church and in Christ Jesus to all generations, forever and ever. Amen.

Conclude by slowly saying the prayer Jesus gave us: the Our Father.

Act

Take some time to read and reflect on the words of Saint John Paul II in his *Letter to Families* (*Gratissimam Sane*) (no. 4): "Prayer makes the Son of God present among us: 'For where two or three are gathered in my name, I am there among them' (Mt 18:20). . . . Prayer increases the strength and spiritual unity of the family, helping the family to partake of God's own 'strength.'" [*]

---

[*] The citation is from http://www.vatican.va/holy_father/john_paul_ii/letters/documents/hf_jp-ii_let_02021994_families_en.html (accessed on 9/16/14). If you have access to the internet, read all of section 4.

PART ONE

Bright Spots and Shadows for the Family Today

The need to understand the situation

4. Since God's plan for marriage and the family touches men and women in the concreteness of their daily existence in specific social and cultural situations, the Church ought to apply herself to understanding the situations within which marriage and the family are lived today, in order to fulfill her task of serving.[8]

This understanding is, therefore, an inescapable requirement of the work of evangelization. It is, in fact, to the families of our times that the Church must bring the unchangeable and ever new Gospel of Jesus Christ, just as it is the families involved in the present conditions of the world that are called to accept and to live the plan of God that pertains to them. Moreover, the call and demands of the Spirit resound in the very events of history, and so the Church can also be guided to a more profound understanding of the inexhaustible mystery of marriage and the family by the circumstances, the questions and the anxieties and hopes of the young people, married couples, and parents of today.[9]

To this ought to be added a further reflection of particular importance at the present time. Not infrequently ideas and solutions which are very appealing but which obscure in varying degrees the truth and the dignity of the human person are offered to the men and women of today, in their sincere and deep search for a response to the important daily problems that affect their married and family life. These views are often supported by the powerful and pervasive organization of the means of social communication, which subtly endanger freedom and the capacity for objective judgment.

Many are already aware of this danger to the human person and are working for the truth. The Church, with her evangelical discernment, joins with them, offering her own service to the truth, to freedom, and to the dignity of every man and every woman.

Evangelical discernment

5. The discernment effected by the Church becomes the offering of an orientation in order that the entire truth and the full dignity of marriage and the family may be preserved and realized.

This discernment is accomplished through the sense of faith[10] which is a gift that the Spirit gives to all the faithful,[11] and is therefore the work of the whole Church according to the diversity of the various gifts and charisms that, together with and according to the responsibility proper to each one, work together for a more profound understanding and activation of the word of God The Church, therefore, does not accomplish this discernment only through the pastors, who teach in the name and with the power of Christ, but also through the laity: Christ "made them his witnesses and gave them understanding of the faith and the grace of speech (cf. Acts 2:17–18; Rev 19:10), so that the power of the Gospel might shine forth in their daily social and family life."[12] The laity, moreover, by reason of their particular vocation, have the specific role of interpreting the history of the world in the light of Christ, in as much as they are called to illuminate and organize temporal realities according to the plan of God, Creator and Redeemer.

The "supernatural sense of faith,"[13] however, does not consist solely or necessarily in the consensus of the faithful. Following Christ, the Church seeks the truth, which is not always the same as the majority opinion. She listens to conscience and not to power, and in this way she defends the poor and the downtrodden. The Church values sociological and statistical research, when it proves helpful in understanding the historical context in which pastoral action has to be developed, and when it leads to a better understanding of the truth. Such research alone, however, is not to be considered in itself an expression of the sense of faith.

Because it is the task of the apostolic ministry to ensure that the Church remains in the truth of Christ and to lead her ever more deeply into that truth, the pastors must promote the sense of the faith in all the faithful, examine and authoritatively judge the genuineness of its expressions, and educate the faithful in an ever more mature evangelical discernment.[14]

Christian spouses and parents can and should offer their unique and irreplaceable contribution to the elaboration of an authentic evangelical discernment in the various situations and cultures in which men and women live their marriage and their family life. They are qualified for this role by their charism or specific gift, the gift of the sacrament of Matrimony.[15]

The situation of the family in the world today

6. The situation in which the family finds itself presents positive and negative aspects: the first are a sign of the salvation of Christ operating in the world; the second, a sign of the refusal that man gives to the love of God.

On the one hand, in fact, there is a more lively awareness of personal freedom and greater attention to the quality of interpersonal relationships in marriage, to promoting the dignity of women, to responsible procreation, to the education of children. There is also an awareness of the need for the development of interfamily relationships, for reciprocal spiritual and material assistance, the rediscovery of the ecclesial mission proper to the family, and its responsibility for the building of a more just society. On the other hand, however, signs are not lacking of a disturbing degradation of some fundamental values: a mistaken theoretical and practical concept of the independence of the spouses in relation to each other, serious misconceptions regarding the relationship of authority between parents and children, the concrete difficulties that the family itself experiences in the transmission of values, the growing number of divorces, the scourge of abortion, the ever more frequent recourse to sterilization, the appearance of a truly contraceptive mentality.

At the root of these negative phenomena there frequently lies a corruption of the idea and the experience of freedom, conceived not as a capacity for realizing the truth of God's plan for marriage and the family, but as an autonomous power of self-affirmation, often against others, for one's own selfish well-being.

Worthy of our attention also is the fact that, in the countries of the so-called Third World, families often lack both the means necessary for survival, such as food, work, housing, and medicine, and the most elementary freedoms. In the richer countries, on the contrary, excessive prosperity and the consumer mentality, paradoxically joined to a certain anguish and uncertainty about the future, deprive married couples of the generosity and courage needed for raising up new human life: thus life is often perceived not as a blessing, but as a danger from which to defend oneself.

The historical situation in which the family lives therefore appears as an interplay of light and darkness.

This shows that history is not simply a fixed progression toward what is better, but rather an event of freedom, and even a struggle between freedoms that are in mutual conflict, that is, according to the well-known expression of Saint Augustine, a conflict between two loves: the love of God to the point of disregarding self, and the love of self to the point of disregarding God.[16]

It follows that only an education for love rooted in faith can lead to the capacity of interpreting "the signs of the times," which are the historical expression of this twofold love.

The influence of circumstances on the consciences of the faithful

7. Living in such a world, under the pressures coming above all from the mass media, the faithful do not always remain immune from the obscuring of certain fundamental values, nor set themselves up as the critical conscience of family culture and as active agents in the building of an authentic family humanism.

Among the more troubling signs of this phenomenon, the Synod fathers stressed the following, in particular: the spread of divorce and of recourse to a new union, even on the part of the faithful; the acceptance of purely civil marriage in contradiction to the vocation of the baptized to "be married in the Lord"; the celebration of the marriage sacrament without living faith, but for other motives; the rejection of the moral norms that guide and promote the human and Christian exercise of sexuality in marriage.

Our age needs wisdom

8. The whole Church is obliged to a deep reflection and commitment, so that the new culture now emerging may be

evangelized in depth, true values acknowledged, the rights of men and women defended, and justice promoted in the very structures of society. In this way the "new humanism" will not distract people from their relationship with God, but will lead them to it more fully.

Science and its technical applications offer new and immense possibilities in the construction of such a humanism. Still, as a consequence of political choices that decide the direction of research and its applications, science is often used against its original purpose, which is the advancement of the human person.

It becomes necessary, therefore, on the part of all, to recover an awareness of the primacy of moral values, which are the values of the human person as such. The great task that has to be faced today for the renewal of society is that of recapturing the ultimate meaning of life and its fundamental values. Only an awareness of the primacy of these values enables man to use the immense possibilities given him by science in such a way as to bring about the true advancement of the human person in his or her whole truth, in his or her freedom and dignity. Science is called to ally itself with wisdom.

The following words of the Second Vatican Council can therefore be applied to the problems of the family: "Our era needs such wisdom more than bygone ages if the discoveries made by man are to be further humanized. For the future of the world stands in peril unless wiser people are forthcoming."[17]

The education of the moral conscience, which makes every human being capable of judging and of discerning the proper ways to achieve self-realization according to his or her original truth, thus becomes a pressing requirement that cannot be renounced.

Modern culture must be led to a more profoundly restored covenant with divine Wisdom. Every man is given a share of such Wisdom through the creating action of God. And it is only in faithfulness to this covenant that the families of today will be in a position to influence positively the building of a more just and fraternal world.

Gradualness and conversion

9. To the injustice originating from sin—which has profoundly penetrated the structures of today's world—and often hindering the family's full realization of itself and of its fundamental rights, we must all set ourselves in opposition through a conversion of mind and heart, following Christ Crucified by denying our own selfishness: such a conversion cannot fail to have a beneficial and renewing influence even on the structures of society.

What is needed is a continuous, permanent conversion which, while requiring an interior detachment from every evil and an adherence to good in its fullness, is brought about concretely in steps which lead us ever forward. Thus a dynamic process develops, one which advances gradually with the progressive integration of the gifts of God and the demands of his definitive and absolute love in the entire personal and social life of man. Therefore an educational growth process is necessary, in order that individual believers, families and peoples, even civilization itself, by beginning from what they have already received of the mystery of Christ, may patiently be led forward, arriving at a richer understanding and a fuller integration of this mystery in their lives.

Inculturation

10. In conformity with her constant tradition, the Church receives from the various cultures everything that is able to express better the unsearchable riches of Christ.[18] Only with the help of all the cultures will it be possible for these riches to be manifested ever more clearly, and for the Church to progress toward a daily more complete and profound awareness of the truth, which has already been given to her in its entirety by the Lord.

Holding fast to the two principles of the compatibility with the Gospel of the various cultures to be taken up, and of communion with the universal Church, there must be further study, particularly by the episcopal conferences and the appropriate departments of the Roman Curia, and greater pastoral diligence so that this "inculturation" of the Christian faith may come about ever more extensively, in the context of marriage and the family as well as in other fields.

It is by means of "inculturation" that one proceeds toward the full restoration of the covenant with the Wisdom of God, which is Christ himself. The whole Church will be enriched also by the cultures which, though lacking technology, abound in human wisdom and are enlivened by profound moral values.

So that the goal of this journey might be clear and consequently the way plainly indicated, the Synod was right to begin by considering in depth the original design of God for marriage and the family: it "went back to the beginning," in deference to the teaching of Christ.[19]

Ponder

In its *Pastoral Constitution on the Church in the Modern World*, the fathers of the Second Vatican Council took up the challenge Jesus addressed to his opponents to "read the signs of the times" (see Mt 16:1–4). Thus *Gaudium et Spes* teaches that: "the Church has always had the duty of scrutinizing the signs of the times and of interpreting them in the light of the Gospel."* The Council used this method of critical discernment to examine positive and negative developments in the modern world.

As Pope, Saint John Paul II continued to use this method of "evangelical discernment." Here he uses it to examine positive and negative developments affecting the life of modern families. He challenges the myth, widespread in Western thinking since the Enlightenment, "that history is . . . a fixed progression toward what is better." Instead it is often a struggle between opposing concepts of freedom or ultimately (with Saint Augustine) between opposing loves—"love of God to the point of disregarding self, and the love of self to the point of disregarding God" (*FC* no. 6).† This ongoing struggle

---

* *Gaudium et Spes*, no. 4. The citation is from http://www.vatican.va/archive/hist_councils/ii_vatican_council/documents/vat-ii_cons_19651207_gaudium-et-spes_en.html (accessed 9/9/14).

† John Paul II is here quoting *The City of God*, XIV, 28.

within human history, culture, and the human heart is an idea to which the Pope would often return.

For John Paul II, the answer to the challenge posed by these clashing loves is the in-depth evangelization of the newly emerging culture of the modern world (see *FC* no. 8). This evangelization requires an encounter with the person of Christ. He would later teach that this was the very purpose of the Church: "*In order to make this 'encounter' with Christ possible, God willed his Church.* Indeed, the Church 'wishes to serve this single end: that each person may be able to find Christ, in order that Christ may walk with each person the path of life.'"[*] This was why he summoned the Church to embark on the new evangelization.

His successors have repeated this summons even more forcefully. In May 2011, Pope Benedict XVI established a new Pontifical Council for Promoting the New Evangelization. Pope Francis has made this effort a focus for the whole of his ministry, beginning his first apostolic exhortation with the words:

> The joy of the gospel fills the hearts and lives of all who encounter Jesus. Those who accept his offer of salvation are set free from sin, sorrow, inner emptiness, and loneliness. With Christ joy is constantly born anew. In this Exhortation I wish to encourage the Christian faithful to embark upon a new chapter of evangelization marked

---

[*] John Paul II, Encyclical Letter *Veritatis Splendor*, no. 7. The citation is from http://www.vatican.va/holy_father/john_paul_ii/encyclicals/documents/hf_jp-ii_enc_06081993_veritatis-splendor_en.html (accessed 9/9/14).

by this joy, while pointing out new paths for the Church's journey in years to come.†

This encouragement is given to the whole Church and in a particular way to its families.

1. What "bright spots" and "shadows" do you see confronting the families around you? What strengths and challenges do you see facing your own family?

2. How have you seen God's grace working to bring about a gradual conversion in your life? Where have you seen this process in the life of your family?

3. Read the account of the first disciples in the Gospel of John 1:35–51. How did they invite others to encounter Jesus? How could you do the same as an individual or as a family?

Pray

The bishops of the United States offer this prayer for the new evangelization:

> For "everyone who calls on the name of the Lord will be saved." But how can they call on him in whom they have not believed? And how can they believe in him of whom they have not heard? And how can they hear without someone to preach? And how can people preach unless they are sent? (Rom 10:13–15)

---

† Pope Francis, *Evangelii Gaudium*, no. 1.

Heavenly Father, pour forth your Holy Spirit to inspire me with these words from Holy Scripture.

Stir in my soul the desire to renew my faith and deepen my relationship with your Son, our Lord Jesus Christ, so that I might truly believe in and live the Good News.

Open my heart to hear the Gospel and grant me the confidence to proclaim the Good News to others.

Pour out your Spirit, so that I might be strengthened to go forth and witness to the Gospel in my everyday life through my words and actions.

In moments of hesitation, remind me:

If not me, then who will proclaim the Gospel?

If not now, then when will the Gospel be proclaimed?

If not the truth of the Gospel, then what shall I proclaim?

God, our Father, I pray that through the Holy Spirit I might hear the call of the new evangelization to deepen my faith, grow in confidence to proclaim the Gospel, and boldly witness to the saving grace of your Son, Jesus Christ, who lives and reigns with you, in the unity of the Holy Spirit, one God, for ever and ever. Amen.[*]

---

[*] The prayer is available on the USCCB Web site at: http://www.usccb.org/prayer-and-worship/prayers-and-devotions/prayers/new-evangelization-prayer.cfm (accessed 9/13/14).

Act

Pray the above prayer again slowly in relation to your family, so that your family might more deeply encounter Christ and that you can bring him to others.

PART TWO

The Plan of God for Marriage and the Family

Man, the image of the God who is Love

11. God created man in his own image and likeness:[20] calling him to existence *through love*, he called him at the same time *for love*.

God is love[21] and in himself he lives a mystery of personal loving communion. Creating the human race in his own image and continually keeping it in being, God inscribed in the humanity of man and woman the vocation, and thus the capacity and responsibility, of love and communion.[22] Love is therefore the fundamental and innate vocation of every human being.

As an incarnate spirit, that is a soul which expresses itself in a body and a body informed by an immortal spirit, man is called to love in his unified totality. Love includes the human body, and the body is made a sharer in spiritual love.

Christian revelation recognizes two specific ways of realizing the vocation of the human person, in its entirety, to love:

marriage, and virginity or celibacy. Either one is, in its own proper form, an actuation of the most profound truth of man, of his being "created in the image of God."

Consequently, sexuality, by means of which man and woman give themselves to one another through the acts which are proper and exclusive to spouses, is by no means something purely biological, but concerns the innermost being of the human person as such. It is realized in a truly human way only if it is an integral part of the love by which a man and a woman commit themselves totally to one another until death. The total physical self-giving would be a lie if it were not the sign and fruit of a total personal self-giving, in which the whole person, including the temporal dimension, is present: if the person were to withhold something or reserve the possibility of deciding otherwise in the future, by this very fact he or she would not be giving totally.

This totality which is required by conjugal love also corresponds to the demands of responsible fertility. This fertility is directed to the generation of a human being, and so by its nature it surpasses the purely biological order and involves a whole series of personal values. For the harmonious growth of these values a persevering and unified contribution by both parents is necessary.

The only "place" in which this self-giving in its whole truth is made possible is marriage, the covenant of conjugal love freely and consciously chosen, whereby man and woman accept the intimate community of life and love willed by God himself,[23] which only in this light manifests its true meaning.

The institution of marriage is not an undue interference by society or authority, nor the extrinsic imposition of a form. Rather it is an interior requirement of the covenant of conjugal love which is publicly affirmed as unique and exclusive, in order to live in complete fidelity to the plan of God, the Creator. A person's freedom, far from being restricted by this fidelity, is secured against every form of subjectivism or relativism and is made a sharer in creative Wisdom.

Marriage and communion between God and people

12. The communion of love between God and people, a fundamental part of the revelation and faith experience of Israel, finds a meaningful expression in the marriage covenant which is established between a man and a woman.

For this reason the central word of revelation, "God loves his people," is likewise proclaimed through the living and concrete word whereby a man and a woman express their conjugal love. Their bond of love becomes the image and the symbol of the covenant which unites God and his people.[24] And the same sin which can harm the conjugal covenant becomes an image of the infidelity of the people to their God: idolatry is prostitution,[25] infidelity is adultery, disobedience to the law is abandonment of the spousal love of the Lord. But the infidelity of Israel does not destroy the eternal fidelity of the Lord, and therefore the ever faithful love of God is put forward as the model of the relations of faithful love which should exist between spouses.[26]

Jesus Christ, Bridegroom of the Church, and the sacrament of Matrimony

13. The communion between God and his people finds its definitive fulfillment in Jesus Christ, the Bridegroom who loves and gives himself as the Savior of humanity, uniting it to himself as his body.

He reveals the original truth of marriage, the truth of the "beginning,"[27] and, freeing man from his hardness of heart, he makes man capable of realizing this truth in its entirety.

This revelation reaches its definitive fullness in the gift of love which the Word of God makes to humanity in assuming a human nature, and in the sacrifice which Jesus Christ makes of himself on the cross for his bride, the Church. In this sacrifice there is entirely revealed that plan which God has imprinted on the humanity of man and woman since their creation;[28] the marriage of baptized persons thus becomes a real symbol of that new and eternal covenant sanctioned in the blood of Christ. The Spirit which the Lord pours forth gives a new heart, and renders man and woman capable of loving one another as Christ has loved us. Conjugal love reaches that fullness to which it is interiorly ordained, conjugal charity, which is the proper and specific way in which the spouses participate in and are called to live the very charity of Christ, who gave himself on the cross.

In a deservedly famous page, Tertullian has well expressed the greatness of this conjugal life in Christ and its beauty: "How can I ever express the happiness of the marriage that is joined together by the Church strengthened by an offering, sealed by a blessing, announced by angels, and ratified by the Father? . . . How wonderful the bond between two believers with a single hope, a single desire, a single observance, a single service! They are both brethren and both fellow servants; there is no separation between them in spirit or flesh; in fact they are truly two in one flesh and where the flesh is one, one is the spirit."[29]

Receiving and meditating faithfully on the word of God, the Church has solemnly taught and continues to teach that the marriage of the baptized is one of the seven sacraments of the New Covenant.[30]

Indeed, by means of baptism, man and woman are definitively placed within the new and eternal covenant, in the spousal covenant of Christ with the Church. And it is because of this indestructible insertion that the intimate community of conjugal life and love, founded by the Creator,[31] is elevated and assumed into the spousal charity of Christ, sustained and enriched by his redeeming power.

By virtue of the sacramentality of their marriage, spouses are bound to one another in the most profoundly indissoluble manner. Their belonging to each other is the real representation, by means of the sacramental sign, of the very relationship of Christ with the Church.

Spouses are therefore the permanent reminder to the Church of what happened on the cross; they are for one another and for the children witnesses to the salvation in which the sacrament makes them sharers. Of this salvation event marriage, like every sacrament, is a memorial, actuation, and prophecy: "As a memorial, the sacrament gives them the grace and duty of commemorating the great works of God and of bearing witness to them before their children. As actuation, it gives them the grace and duty of putting into practice in the present, toward each other and their children, the demands of a love which forgives and redeems. As prophecy, it gives them the grace and duty of living and bearing witness to the hope of the future encounter with Christ."[32]

Like each of the seven sacraments, so also marriage is a real symbol of the event of salvation, but in its own way. "The spouses participate in it as spouses, together, as a couple, so that the first and immediate effect of marriage (*res et sacramentum*) is not supernatural grace itself, but the Christian conjugal bond, a typically Christian communion of two persons because it represents the mystery of Christ's incarnation and the mystery of his covenant. The content of participation in Christ's life is also specific: conjugal love involves a totality, in which all the elements of the person enter—appeal of the body and instinct, power of feeling and affectivity, aspiration of the spirit and of will. It aims at a deeply personal unity, the unity that, beyond union in one flesh, leads to forming one heart and soul; it demands indissolubility and faithfulness in definitive mutual giving; and it is open to fertility (cf. *Humanae Vitae*, no. 9). In a word it is a question of the normal characteristics of all natural conjugal love, but with a new significance which not only purifies and strengthens them, but raises them to the extent of making them the expression of specifically Christian values."[33]

Children, the precious gift of marriage

14. According to the plan of God, marriage is the foundation of the wider community of the family, since the very institution of marriage and conjugal love are ordained to the procreation and education of children, in whom they find their crowning.[34]

In its most profound reality, love is essentially a gift; and conjugal love, while leading the spouses to the reciprocal "knowledge" which makes them "one flesh,"[35] does not end with the couple, because it makes them capable of the greatest possible gift, the gift by which they become cooperators with God for giving life to a new human person. Thus the couple, while giving themselves to one another, give not just themselves but also the reality of children, who are a living reflection of their love, a permanent sign of conjugal unity, and a living and inseparable synthesis of their being a father and a mother.

When they become parents, spouses receive from God the gift of a new responsibility. Their parental love is called to become for the children the visible sign of the very love of God, "from whom every family in heaven and on earth is named."[36]

It must not be forgotten, however, that even when procreation is not possible, conjugal life does not for this reason lose its value. Physical sterility in fact can be for spouses the occasion for other important services to the life of the human person, for example, adoption, various forms of educational work, and assistance to other families and to poor or handicapped children.

The family, a communion of persons

15. In Matrimony and in the family a complex of inter-personal relationships is set up—married life, fatherhood and motherhood, filiation and fraternity—through which each human person is introduced into the "human family" and into the "family of God," which is the Church.

Christian marriage and the Christian family build up the Church: for in the family the human person is not only brought into being and progressively introduced by means of education into the human community, but by means of the rebirth of baptism and education in the faith the child is also introduced into God's family, which is the Church.

The human family, disunited by sin, is reconstituted in its unity by the redemptive power of the death and resurrection of Christ.[37] Christian marriage, by participating in the salvific efficacy of this event, constitutes the natural setting in which the human person is introduced into the great family of the Church.

The commandment to grow and multiply, given to man and woman in the beginning, in this way reaches its whole truth and full realization.

The Church thus finds in the family, born from the sacrament, the cradle and the setting in which she can enter the human generations, and where these in their turn can enter the Church.

Marriage and virginity or celibacy

16. Virginity or celibacy for the sake of the Kingdom of God not only does not contradict the dignity of marriage but presupposes it and confirms it. Marriage and virginity or celibacy are two ways of expressing and living the one mystery of the covenant of God with his people. When marriage is not esteemed, neither can consecrated virginity or celibacy exist; when human sexuality is not regarded as a great value given by the Creator, the renunciation of it for the sake of the Kingdom of Heaven loses its meaning.

Rightly indeed does Saint John Chrysostom say: "Whoever denigrates marriage also diminishes the glory of virginity. Whoever praises it makes virginity more admirable and resplendent. What appears good only in comparison with evil would not be particularly good. It is something better than what is admitted to be good that is the most excellent good."[38]

In virginity or celibacy, the human being is awaiting, also in a bodily way, the eschatological marriage of Christ with the Church, giving himself or herself completely to the Church in the hope that Christ may give himself to the Church in the full truth of eternal life. The celibate person thus anticipates in his or her flesh the new world of the future resurrection.[39]

By virtue of this witness, virginity or celibacy keeps alive in the Church a consciousness of the mystery of marriage and defends it from any reduction and impoverishment.

Virginity or celibacy, by liberating the human heart in a unique way,[40] "so as to make it burn with greater love for God and all humanity,"[41] bears witness that the Kingdom of God and his justice is that pearl of great price which is preferred to every other value no matter how great, and hence must be sought as the only definitive value. It is for this reason that the Church, throughout her history, has always defended the superiority of this charism to that of marriage, by reason of the wholly singular link which it has with the Kingdom of God.[42]

In spite of having renounced physical fecundity, the celibate person becomes spiritually fruitful, the father and mother of many, cooperating in the realization of the family according to God's plan.

Christian couples therefore have the right to expect from celibate persons a good example and a witness of fidelity to their vocation until death. Just as fidelity at times becomes difficult for married people and requires sacrifice, mortification, and self-denial, the same can happen to celibate persons, and their fidelity, even in the trials that may occur, should strengthen the fidelity of married couples.[43]

These reflections on virginity or celibacy can enlighten and help those who, for reasons independent of their own will, have been unable to marry and have then accepted their situation in a spirit of service.

Ponder

"God created man in his own image and likeness: calling him to existence *through love*, he called him at the same time *for love*" (*FC* no. 11). With these words, we arrive at the theological heart of Saint John Paul II's teaching on the family. The reason for our creation, for our redemption by Christ, for our call to the glory of heaven is so that we might reflect and experience the reality of who God is: love.

But neither God nor the human person who is his image is a solitary being. God is an eternal communion of love. The three Divine Persons of the Father, Son, and Holy Spirit—each of whom is equally and fully God—live in a ceaseless union of total self-gift to one another. John Paul II describes this mystery of God's own life as a "communion of Persons." In creation this communion is reflected in the duality of male and female, who come together in love in the covenant of marriage. Their love expressed in the bodily gift of themselves to one another is ordered to life—children (whether natural or adopted) complete and express in a new way the love between husband and wife. As he would later write in his *Letter to Families*: "the 'communion' of the spouses gives rise to the 'community' of the family" and in turn the " 'community' of the family is completely pervaded by the very essence of 'communion.'"* Marriage and the family can be a

---

* *Gratissimam Sane*, no. 7.

"communion of persons" in which each person lives for the others, an icon of the Trinity on earth.

In salvation history the covenant of marriage becomes part of the grammar by which God communicates his love to his people. God's covenant with the people of Israel in the Old Testament is described as a marriage. In the New Testament, Jesus, who is the Father's final and definitive Word of love, is the Bridegroom who lays down his life to redeem his bride, the Church (see Eph 5:21–33).

This same eternal and unbreakable love is the source and animating principle within Christian marriage. In it the natural love and attraction of the sexes, wounded by sin, is healed, elevated, and transformed. The water of frail human effort is replaced by the new and excellent wine of grace, communicated to the couple by the Holy Spirit in the Church's sacramental life (see Jn 2:1–11). The unbreakable nature of Christ's love enables Christian marriage to also be unbreakable or "indissoluble," empowering spouses to be a living sign of divine love in the world.

The other primary way in which Christians respond to the human vocation to love is in consecrated virginity or religious celibacy. Here too men and women live the "sincere gift of self" by giving themselves to God and the Church by means of their bodies.[*] In so doing they bear witness to "the eschatological marriage of Christ with the Church" (*FC* no. 16), and provide a precious witness of the priority of God's love to the Church and to the world.

---

[*] The phrase is from *Gaudium et Spes*, no. 24.

1. What does it mean to you to say that the meaning and purpose of your existence is love? How do you see your body and its sexuality as an integral part of that reality?

2. Why does John Paul II teach that the only "place" where sexual "self-giving in its whole truth is made possible is marriage, the covenant of conjugal love freely and consciously chosen" (*FC* no. 11)? What has been the fruit of the widespread rejection of this teaching in the culture around us?

3. How can understanding Christian marriage as a participation in the unbreakable love of Christ for the Church provide encouragement to couples when they face challenges in their own marriages? What are ways that couples can draw on the grace available to them in the sacrament?

4. How do marriage and consecrated virginity support and reinforce one another in drawing attention to our call to love? What can be done to repair the harm done by the scandals caused by people's failure to faithfully live these vocations?

Pray

The word "vocation" comes from the Latin *vocare* ("to call"). Pray this prayer for an increase of vocations in the Church (or a prayer from your own heart):

Heavenly Father,
You desire all of your children to be happy.

You created each one of us out of love to bring your love to others.

Give us the grace to respond to your call to us and choose the vocation that you know is best for us.

Help us to treasure the gift of marriage, which reflects the love of Christ for the Church.

Empower us to uphold the institution of marriage in our society as the place where love is nurtured and family life begins.

Raise up more holy Christian marriages and strong families, which bear witness to your love in the world.

Stir up the grace of religious vocation in the hearts of many men and women.

Grant them generous hearts to give their time, talents, and very selves in the service of your holy Church.

Act

Compose a "prayer of the faithful" that asks God for an increase of vocations to priesthood and religious life *and* vibrant Christian marriages. Ask your pastor or liturgy team to consider using it at Mass.

PART THREE

The Role of the Christian Family

Family, become what you are

17. The family finds in the plan of God the Creator and Redeemer not only its *identity*, what it *is*, but also its *mission*, what it can and should *do*. The role that God calls the family to perform in history derives from what the family is; its role represents the dynamic and existential development of what it is. Each family finds within itself a summons that cannot be ignored, and that specifies both its dignity and its responsibility: family, *become* what you *are*.

Accordingly, the family must go back to the "beginning" of God's creative act, if it is to attain self-knowledge and self-realization in accordance with the inner truth not only of what it is but also of what it does in history. And since in God's plan it has been established as an "intimate community of life and love,"[44] the family has the mission to become more and more what it is, that is to say, a community of life and love, in an effort that will find fulfillment, as will everything created and redeemed, in the Kingdom of God. Looking at it in such a way as to reach its very roots, we must say that the essence and role of the family are in the final analysis specified by love. Hence the family has *the mission to guard, reveal, and communicate love*, and this is a living reflection of and a real sharing in God's love for humanity and the love of Christ the Lord for the Church his bride.

Every particular task of the family is an expression and concrete actuation of that fundamental mission. We must therefore go deeper into the unique riches of the family's mission and probe its contents, which are both manifold and unified.

Thus, with love as its point of departure and making constant reference to it, the recent Synod emphasized four general tasks for the family:

1) forming a community of persons;

2) serving life;

3) participating in the development of society;

4) sharing in the life and mission of the Church.

I. Forming a Community of Persons

Love as the principle and power of communion

18. The family, which is founded and given life by love, is a community of persons: of husband and wife, of parents and children, of relatives. Its first task is to live with fidelity the reality of communion in a constant effort to develop an authentic community of persons.

The inner principle of that task, its permanent power and its final goal is love: without love the family is not a community of persons and, in the same way, *without love the family cannot live, grow, and perfect itself as a community of persons.* What I wrote in the Encyclical *Redemptor Hominis* applies primarily and especially within the family as such: "Man cannot live without love. He remains a being that is incomprehensible for himself, his life is senseless, if love is not revealed to him, if he does not encounter love, if he does not experience it and make it his own, if he does not participate intimately in it."[45]

The love between husband and wife and, in a derivatory and broader way, the love between members of the same family—between parents and children, brothers and sisters, and relatives and members of the household—is given life and sustenance by an unceasing inner dynamism leading the family to ever deeper and more intense *communion*, which is the foundation and soul of the *community* of marriage and the family.

The indivisible unity of conjugal communion

19. The first communion is the one which is established and which develops between husband and wife: by virtue of the covenant of married life, the man and woman "are no longer two but one flesh,"[46] and they are called to grow continually in their communion through day-to-day fidelity to their marriage promise of total mutual self-giving.

This conjugal communion sinks its roots in the natural complementarity that exists between man and woman, and is nurtured through the personal willingness of the spouses to share their entire life project, what they have and what they are: for this reason such communion is the fruit and the sign of a profoundly human need. But in Christ the Lord, God takes up this human need, confirms it, purifies it, and elevates it, leading it to perfection through the sacrament of Matrimony: the Holy Spirit who is poured out in the sacramental celebration offers Christian couples the gift of a new communion of love that is the living and real image of that unique unity which makes of the Church the indivisible Mystical Body of the Lord Jesus.

The gift of the Spirit is a commandment of life for Christian spouses and at the same time a stimulating impulse so that every day they may progress toward an ever richer union with each other on all levels—of the body, of the character, of the heart, of the intelligence and will, of the soul[47] —revealing in this way to the Church and to the world the new communion of love, given by the grace of Christ.

Such a communion is radically contradicted by polygamy: this, in fact, directly negates the plan of God which was revealed from the beginning, because it is contrary to the equal personal dignity of men and women who in Matrimony give themselves with a love that is total and therefore unique and exclusive. As the Second Vatican Council writes: "Firmly established by the Lord, the unity of marriage will radiate from the equal personal dignity of husband and wife, a dignity acknowledged by mutual and total love."[48]

An indissoluble communion

20. Conjugal communion is characterized not only by its unity but also by its indissolubility: "As a mutual gift of two persons, this intimate union, as well as the good of children, imposes total fidelity on the spouses and argues for an unbreakable oneness between them."[49]

It is a fundamental duty of the Church to reaffirm strongly, as the Synod Fathers did, the doctrine of the indissolubility of marriage. To all those who, in our times, consider it too difficult, or indeed impossible, to be bound to one person for the whole of life, and to those caught up in a culture that rejects the indissolubility of marriage and openly mocks the commitment of spouses to fidelity, it is necessary to reconfirm the good news of the definitive nature of that conjugal love that has in Christ its foundation and strength.[50]

Being rooted in the personal and total self-giving of the couple, and being required by the good of the children, the indissolubility of marriage finds its ultimate truth in the plan that God has manifested in his revelation: he wills and he communicates the indissolubility of marriage as a fruit, a sign, and a requirement of the absolutely faithful love that God has for man and that the Lord Jesus has for the Church.

Christ renews the first plan that the Creator inscribed in the hearts of man and woman, and in the celebration of the sacrament of Matrimony offers a "new heart": thus the couples are not only able to overcome "hardness of heart,"[51] but also and above all they are able to share the full and definitive love of Christ, the new and eternal Covenant made flesh. Just as the Lord Jesus is the "faithful witness,"[52] the "yes" of the promises of God[53] and thus the supreme realization of the unconditional faithfulness with which God loves his people, so Christian couples are called to participate truly in the irrevocable indissolubility that binds Christ to the Church his bride, loved by him to the end.[54]

The gift of the sacrament is at the same time a vocation and commandment for the Christian spouses, that they may remain faithful to each other forever, beyond every trial and difficulty, in generous obedience to the holy will of the Lord: "What therefore God has joined together, let not man put asunder."[55]

To bear witness to the inestimable value of the indissolubility and fidelity of marriage is one of the most precious and most urgent tasks of Christian couples in our time. So, with all my brothers who participated in the Synod of Bishops, I praise and encourage those numerous couples who, though encountering no small difficulty, preserve and develop the value of indissolubility: thus, in a humble and courageous manner, they perform the role committed to them of being in the world a "sign"—a small and precious sign, sometimes also subjected to temptation, but always renewed—of the unfailing fidelity with which God and Jesus Christ love each and every human being. But it is also proper to recognize the value of the witness of those spouses who, even when abandoned by their partner, with the strength of faith and of Christian hope have not entered a new union: these spouses too give an authentic witness to fidelity, of which the world today has a great need. For this reason they must be encouraged and helped by the pastors and the faithful of the Church.

The broader communion of the family

21. Conjugal communion constitutes the foundation on which is built the broader communion of the family, of parents and children, of brothers and sisters with each other, of relatives and other members of the household.

This communion is rooted in the natural bonds of flesh and blood, and grows to its specifically human perfection with the establishment and maturing of the still deeper and richer bonds of the spirit: the love that animates the interpersonal relationships of the different members of the family constitutes the interior strength that shapes and animates the family communion and community.

The Christian family is also called to experience a new and original communion which confirms and perfects natural and human communion. In fact the grace of Jesus Christ, "the firstborn among many brethren"[56] is by its nature and interior dynamism "a grace of brotherhood," as Saint Thomas Aquinas calls it.[57] The Holy Spirit, who is poured forth in the celebration of the sacraments, is the living source and inexhaustible sustenance of the supernatural communion that gathers believers and links them with Christ and with each other in the unity of the Church of God. The Christian family constitutes a specific revelation and realization of ecclesial communion, and for this reason too it can and should be called "the domestic church."[58]

All members of the family, each according to his or her own gift, have the grace and responsibility of building, day by day, the communion of persons, making the family "a school of deeper humanity":[59] this happens where there is care and love for the little ones, the sick, the aged; where there is mutual service every day; when there is a sharing of goods, of joys, and of sorrows.

A fundamental opportunity for building such a communion is constituted by the educational exchange between parents and children,[60] in which each gives and receives. By means of love, respect, and obedience toward their parents, children offer their specific and irreplaceable contribution to the construction of an authentically human and Christian family.[61] They will be aided in this if parents exercise their unrenounceable authority as a true and proper "ministry," that is, as a service to the human and Christian well-being of their children, and in particular as a service aimed at helping them acquire a truly responsible freedom, and if parents maintain a living awareness of the "gift" they continually receive from their children.

Family communion can only be preserved and perfected through a great spirit of sacrifice. It requires, in fact, a ready and generous openness of each and all to understanding, to forbearance, to pardon, to reconciliation. There is no family that does not know how selfishness, discord, tension, and conflict violently attack and at times mortally wound its own communion: hence there arise the many and varied forms of division in family life. But, at the same time, every family is called by the God of peace to have the joyous and renewing experience of "reconciliation," that is, communion reestablished, unity restored. In particular, participation in the sacrament of Reconciliation and in the banquet of the one

Body of Christ offers to the Christian family the grace and the responsibility of overcoming every division and of moving toward the fullness of communion willed by God, responding in this way to the ardent desire of the Lord: "that they may be one."[62]

The rights and role of women

22. In that it is, and ought always to become, a communion and community of persons, the family finds in love the source and the constant impetus for welcoming, respecting, and promoting each one of its members in his or her lofty dignity as a person, that is, as a living image of God. As the Synod Fathers rightly stated, the moral criterion for the authenticity of conjugal and family relationships consists in fostering the dignity and vocation of the individual persons, who achieve their fullness by sincere self-giving.[63]

In this perspective the Synod devoted special attention to women, to their rights and role within the family and society. In the same perspective are also to be considered men as husbands and fathers, and likewise children and the elderly.

Above all it is important to underline the equal dignity and responsibility of women with men. This equality is realized in a unique manner in that reciprocal self-giving by each one to the other and by both to the children, which is proper to marriage and the family. What human reason intuitively perceives and acknowledges is fully revealed by the word of God: the history of salvation, in fact, is a continuous and luminous testimony of the dignity of women.

In creating the human race "male and female,"[64] God gives man and woman an equal personal dignity, endowing them with the inalienable rights and responsibilities proper to the human person. God then manifests the dignity of women in the highest form possible, by assuming human flesh from the Virgin Mary, whom the Church honors as the Mother of God, calling her the new Eve and presenting her as the model of redeemed woman. The sensitive respect of Jesus toward the women that he called to his following and his friendship, his appearing on Easter morning to a woman before the other disciples, the mission entrusted to women to carry the good news of the resurrection to the apostles—these are all signs that confirm the special esteem of the Lord Jesus for women. The Apostle Paul will say: "In Christ Jesus you are all children of God through faith. . . . There is neither Jew nor Greek, there is neither slave nor free, there is neither male nor female; for you are all one in Christ Jesus."[65]

Women and society

23. Without intending to deal with all the various aspects of the vast and complex theme of the relationships between women and society, and limiting these remarks to a few essential points, one cannot but observe that in the specific area of family life a widespread social and cultural tradition has considered women's role to be exclusively that of wife and mother, without adequate access to public functions which have generally been reserved for men.

There is no doubt that the equal dignity and responsibility of men and women fully justifies women's access to public functions. On the other hand the true advancement of women requires that clear recognition be given to the value of their maternal and family role, by comparison with all other public roles and all other professions. Furthermore, these roles and professions should be harmoniously combined, if we wish the evolution of society and culture to be truly and fully human.

This will come about more easily if, in accordance with the wishes expressed by the Synod, a renewed "theology of work" can shed light upon and study in depth the meaning of work in the Christian life and determine the fundamental bond between work and the family, and therefore the original and irreplaceable meaning of work in the home and in rearing children.[66] Therefore the Church can and should help modern society by tirelessly insisting that the work of women in the home be recognized and respected by all in its irreplaceable value. This is of particular importance in education: for possible discrimination between the different types of work and professions is eliminated at its very root once it is clear that all people, in every area, are working with equal rights and equal responsibilities. The image of God in man and in woman will thus be seen with added luster.

While it must be recognized that women have the same right as men to perform various public functions, society must be structured in such a way that wives and mothers are *not in practice compelled* to work outside the home, and that their families can live and prosper in a dignified way even when they themselves devote their full time to their own family.

Furthermore, the mentality which honors women more for their work outside the home than for their work within the family must be overcome. This requires that men should truly esteem and love women with total respect for their personal dignity, and that society should create and develop conditions favoring work in the home.

With due respect to the different vocations of men and women, the Church must in her own life promote as far as possible their equality of rights and dignity: and this for the good of all, the family, the Church, and society.

But clearly all of this does not mean for women a renunciation of their femininity or an imitation of the male role, but the fullness of true feminine humanity which should be expressed in their activity, whether in the family or outside of it, without disregarding the differences of customs and cultures in this sphere.

Offenses against women's dignity

24. Unfortunately the Christian message about the dignity of women is contradicted by that persistent mentality which considers the human being not as a person but as a thing, as an object of trade, at the service of selfish interest and mere pleasure: the first victims of this mentality are women.

This mentality produces very bitter fruits, such as contempt for men and for women, slavery, oppression of the weak, pornography, prostitution—especially in an organized form

—and all those various forms of discrimination that exist in the fields of education, employment, wages, etc.

Besides, many forms of degrading discrimination still persist today in a great part of our society that affect and seriously harm particular categories of women, as for example childless wives, widows, separated or divorced women, and unmarried mothers.

The Synod Fathers deplored these and other forms of discrimination as strongly as possible. I therefore ask that vigorous and incisive pastoral action be taken by all to overcome them definitively so that the image of God that shines in all human beings without exception may be fully respected.

Men as husbands and fathers

25. Within the conjugal and family communion-community, the man is called upon to live his gift and role as husband and father.

In his wife he sees the fulfillment of God's intention: "It is not good that the man should be alone, I will make him a helper fit for him,"[67] and he makes his own the cry of Adam, the first husband: "This at last is bone of my bones and flesh of my flesh."[68]

Authentic conjugal love presupposes and requires that a man have a profound respect for the equal dignity of his wife: "You are not her master," writes Saint Ambrose, "but her husband; she was not given to you to be your slave, but your wife. . . . Reciprocate her attentiveness to you and be grateful to her for her love."[69] With his wife a man should live "a very special form of personal friendship."[70] As for the Christian, he is called upon to develop a new attitude of love, manifesting toward his wife a charity that is both gentle and strong, like that which Christ has for the Church.[71]

Love for his wife as mother of their children and love for the children themselves are for the man the natural way of understanding and fulfilling his own fatherhood. Above all where social and cultural conditions so easily encourage a father to be less concerned with his family or at any rate less involved in the work of education, efforts must be made to restore socially the conviction that the place and task of the father in and for the family is of unique and irreplaceable importance.[72] As experience teaches, the absence of a father causes psychological and moral imbalance and notable difficulties in family relationships, as does, in contrary circumstances, the oppressive presence of a father, especially where there still prevails the phenomenon of "machismo," or a wrong superiority of male prerogatives which humiliates women and inhibits the development of healthy family relationships.

In revealing and in reliving on earth the very fatherhood of God,[73] a man is called upon to ensure the harmonious and united development of all the members of the family: he will perform this task by exercising generous responsibility for the life conceived under the heart of the mother, by a more solicitous commitment to education, a task he shares with his wife,[74] by work which is never a cause of division in the family but promotes its unity and stability, and by means of the witness he gives of an adult Christian life which effectively introduces the children into the living experience of Christ and the Church.

The rights of children

26. In the family, which is a community of persons, special attention must be devoted to the children by developing a profound esteem for their personal dignity, and a great respect and generous concern for their rights. This is true for every child, but it becomes all the more urgent the smaller the child is and the more it is in need of everything, when it is sick, suffering, or handicapped.

By fostering and exercising a tender and strong concern for every child that comes into this world, the Church fulfills a fundamental mission: for she is called upon to reveal and put forward anew in history the example and the commandment of Christ the Lord, who placed the child at the heart of the Kingdom of God: "Let the children come to me, and do not hinder them; for to such belongs the kingdom of heaven."[75]

I repeat once again what I said to the General Assembly of the United Nations on October 2, 1979: "I wish to express the joy that we all find in children, the springtime of life, the anticipation of the future history of each of our present earthly homelands. No country on earth, no political system can think of its own future otherwise than through the image of these new generations that will receive from their parents the manifold heritage of values, duties, and aspirations of the nation to which they belong and of the whole human family. Concern for the child, even before birth, from the first moment of conception and then throughout the years of infancy and youth, is the primary and fundamental test of the relationship of one human being to another. And so, what better wish can I express for every nation and for the whole of mankind, and for all the children of the world than a better future in which respect for human rights will become a complete reality throughout the third millennium, which is drawing near?"[76]

Acceptance, love, esteem, many-sided and united material, emotional, educational, and spiritual concern for every child that comes into this world should always constitute a distinctive, essential characteristic of all Christians, in particular of the Christian family: thus children, while they are able to grow "in wisdom and in stature, and in favor with God and man,"[77] offer their own precious contribution to building up the family community and even to the sanctification of their parents.[78]

The elderly in the family

27. There are cultures which manifest a unique veneration and great love for the elderly: far from being outcasts from the family or merely tolerated as a useless burden, they continue to be present and to take an active and responsible part in family life, though having to respect the autonomy of the new family; above all they carry out the important mission of being a witness to the past and a source of wisdom for the young and for the future.

Other cultures, however, especially in the wake of disordered industrial and urban development, have both in the past and in the present set the elderly aside in unacceptable ways. This causes acute suffering to them and spiritually impoverishes many families.

The pastoral activity of the Church must help everyone to discover and to make good use of the role of the elderly within the civil and ecclesial community, in particular within the family. In fact, "the life of the aging helps to clarify a scale of human values; it shows the continuity of generations and marvelously demonstrates the interdependence of God's people. The elderly often have the charism to bridge generation gaps before they are made: how many children have found understanding and love in the eyes and words and caresses of the aging! And how many old people have willingly subscribed to the inspired word that the 'crown of the aged is their children's children' (Prv 17:6)!"[79]

Ponder

Having described the dignity and vocation of the human person as love, Saint John Paul II now applies this in a particular way to the family. He teaches that the family "has *the mission to guard, reveal, and communicate love*" (*FC* no. 17). The first way in which it does this is to form a communion of persons.

The inner principle and animating force of all that the family does is love: "*without love the family cannot live, grow, and perfect itself as a community of persons*" (*FC* no. 18). This love and the communion it creates are rooted in the unity of husband and wife. The importance of this unity creates moral responsibilities for families and for the society in which they live. Hence marriage must be protected from threats such as polygamy, infidelity, and divorce, which radically contradict its fidelity and indissolubility. Families must also be protected from more subtle daily threats such as inattention, resentment, and selfishness. They therefore have a constant duty to seek " 'reconciliation,' that is, communion reestablished, unity restored" in the sacrament of Reconciliation, participation in the Eucharist, and in their own daily prayer and life together as the "domestic church" (*FC* no. 21).

This communion of love that families are meant to embody rests in turn on respect for the dignity of those within it— men, women, children, the elderly. Recognizing the new position of women in the twentieth century, the Pope devotes particular attention to the rights and dignity of women. Created in the image and likeness of God in the beginning and incorporated into the redeeming mission of Jesus, women enjoy equal dignity with men. He advocates balancing women's equal "right as men to perform various public functions" in the economic or political sphere with their irreplaceable contribution within the home as wives and mothers (*FC* no. 23). This means valuing the contribution made by work in the home and offering what he described elsewhere as: "a *family wage*—that is, a single salary given to the head of the family for his work, sufficient for the needs of the family without the other spouse having to take up gainful employment outside the home."[*]

In later writings, expanding this call to recognize women's dignity, he affirmed "that 'genius' which belongs to women"[†]and called for "a new feminism" in which women themselves articulated their distinctive gifts and contributions to family and society.[‡] The more brief exhortation given to men to honor the equal dignity and unique gifts of their wives

---

[*] John Paul II, Encyclical Letter *Laborem Exercens* (1981), no. 19. The citation is from http://www.vatican.va/holy_father/john_paul_ii/encyclicals/documents/hf_jp-ii_enc_14091981_laborem-exercens_en.html (accessed 9/13/14).

[†]The phrase is found in his Apostolic Letter *Mulieris Dignitatem* (1988), no. 30. The citation is from http://www.vatican.va/holy_father/john_paul_ii/apost_letters/documents/hf_jp-ii_apl_15081988_mulieris-dignitatem_en.html (accessed 9/13/14).

[‡] See the Encyclical Letter *Evangelium Vitae*, no. 99.

(see *FC* no. 25) would later become a development of the Catholic understanding of marriage. John Paul II taught that the authority in marriage must be "carried out in a new way: as a *'mutual subjection out of reverence for Christ'* (cf. Eph 5:21)."* His words decrying offenses to women's dignity, such as human trafficking and pornography, ring even more true in our own day with the spread of these vicious practices throughout our culture.

1. In his work as a Catholic philosopher, Karol Wojtyła, articulated a tool for respecting human dignity in action that he called "the personalistic norm"—the idea that persons should be loved rather than used. That is, they ought to be treated as ends in themselves rather than as a means to an end. How can this principle be applied to the relationship of husbands and wives in marriage?

2. Describe some of the unique gifts and contributions that women offer to the economic, political, and cultural life of society in our day.

3. What does it mean to you to say that husbands and wives exercise mutual authority in marriage? Identify a concrete example of this in practice that you have observed in your own marriage or those of others.

4. In his *Letter to Families* (no. 15) John Paul II also discussed the need for mutual honor between parents and

---

* *Mulieris Dignitatem*, no. 24.

children. He taught that this underscores the need for parents to listen to and acknowledge their children. Can you think of other examples of this principle?

Pray

Read Psalm 8 and prayerfully reflect on your dignity as a person created in the image and likeness of God. Now read the account of the greatest commandment and the Good Samaritan in the Gospel of Luke (10:25–37). In light of the parable, what does it mean to love your neighbor as yourself? Ask our Lord to show you how you can more fully live out this commandment in your relationships.

Act

Make a conscious effort to affirm the dignity of all of the persons with whom you interact today—especially the members of your family.

II. Serving Life

1. The transmission of life

Cooperators in the love of God the Creator

28. With the creation of man and woman in his own image and likeness, God crowns and brings to perfection the work of his hands: he calls them to a special sharing in his love and in his power as Creator and Father, through their free and responsible cooperation in transmitting the gift of human life: "God blessed them, and God said to them, 'Be fruitful and multiply, and fill the earth and subdue it.'"[80]

Thus the fundamental task of the family is to serve life, to actualize in history the original blessing of the Creator—that of transmitting by procreation the divine image from person to person.[81]

Fecundity is the fruit and the sign of conjugal love, the living testimony of the full reciprocal self-giving of the spouses: "While not making the other purposes of Matrimony of less account, the true practice of conjugal love, and the whole meaning of the family life which results from it, have this aim: that the couple be ready with stout hearts to cooperate with the love of the Creator and the Savior, who through them will enlarge and enrich his own family day by day."[82]

However, the fruitfulness of conjugal love is not restricted solely to the procreation of children, even understood in its specifically human dimension: it is enlarged and enriched by all those fruits of moral, spiritual, and supernatural life which the father and mother are called to hand on to their children, and through the children to the Church and to the world.

The Church's teaching and norm, always old yet always new

29. Precisely because the love of husband and wife is a unique participation in the mystery of life and of the love of God himself, the Church knows that she has received the special mission of guarding and protecting the lofty dignity of marriage and the most serious responsibility of the transmission of human life.

Thus, in continuity with the living tradition of the ecclesial community throughout history, the recent Second Vatican Council and the Magisterium of my predecessor Paul VI, expressed above all in the Encyclical *Humanae Vitae*, have handed on to our times a truly prophetic proclamation, which reaffirms and reproposes with clarity the Church's teaching and norm, always old yet always new, regarding marriage and regarding the transmission of human life.

For this reason the Synod Fathers made the following declaration at their last assembly: "This Sacred Synod, gathered together with the Successor of Peter in the unity of faith, firmly holds what has been set forth in the Second Vatican Council (cf. *Gaudium et Spes*, no. 50) and afterward in the Encyclical *Humanae Vitae*, particularly that love between husband and wife must be fully human, exclusive, and open to new life (*Humanae Vitae*, no. 11; cf. nos. 9, 12)."[83]

The Church stands for life

30. The teaching of the Church in our day is placed in a social and cultural context which renders it more difficult to understand and yet more urgent and irreplaceable for promoting the true good of men and women.

Scientific and technical progress, which contemporary man is continually expanding in his dominion over nature, not only offers the hope of creating a new and better humanity, but also causes ever greater anxiety regarding the future. Some ask themselves if it is a good thing to be alive or if it would be better never to have been born; they doubt therefore if it is right to bring others into life when perhaps they will curse their existence in a cruel world with unforeseeable terrors. Others consider themselves to be the only ones for whom the advantages of technology are intended, and they exclude others by imposing on them contraceptives or even worse means. Still others, imprisoned in a consumer mentality and whose sole concern is to bring about a continual growth of material goods, finish by ceasing to understand, and thus by refusing, the spiritual riches of a new human life. The ultimate reason for these mentalities is the absence in people's hearts of God, whose love alone is stronger than all the world's fears and can conquer them.

Thus an anti-life mentality is born, as can be seen in many current issues: one thinks, for example, of a certain panic deriving from the studies of ecologists and futurologists on population growth, which sometimes exaggerate the danger of demographic increase to the quality of life.

But the Church firmly believes that human life, even if weak and suffering, is always a splendid gift of God's goodness. Against the pessimism and selfishness which cast a shadow over the world, the Church stands for life: in each human life she sees the splendor of that "Yes," that "Amen," who is Christ himself.[84] To the "No" which assails and afflicts the world, she replies with this living "Yes," thus defending the human person and the world from all who plot against and harm life.

The Church is called upon to manifest anew to everyone, with clear and stronger conviction, her will to promote human life by every means and to defend it against all attacks, in whatever condition or state of development it is found.

Thus the Church condemns as a grave offense against human dignity and justice all those activities of governments or other public authorities which attempt to limit in any way the freedom of couples in deciding about children. Consequently, any violence applied by such authorities in favor of contraception or, still worse, of sterilization and procured abortion, must be altogether condemned and forcefully rejected. Likewise to be denounced as gravely unjust are cases where, in international relations, economic help given for the advancement of peoples is made conditional on programs of contraception, sterilization, and procured abortion.[85]

That God's design may be ever more completely fulfilled

31. The Church is certainly aware of the many complex problems which couples in many countries face today in their

task of transmitting life in a responsible way. She also recognizes the serious problem of population growth in the form it has taken in many parts of the world and its moral implications.

However, she holds that consideration in depth of all the aspects of these problems offers a new and stronger confirmation of the importance of the authentic teaching on birth regulation reproposed in the Second Vatican Council and in the Encyclical *Humanae Vitae*.

For this reason, together with the Synod Fathers I feel it is my duty to extend a pressing invitation to theologians, asking them to unite their efforts in order to collaborate with the hierarchical Magisterium and to commit themselves to the task of illustrating ever more clearly the biblical foundations, the ethical grounds, and the personalistic reasons behind this doctrine. Thus it will be possible, in the context of an organic exposition, to render the teaching of the Church on this fundamental question truly accessible to all people of good will, fostering a daily more enlightened and profound understanding of it: in this way God's plan will be ever more completely fulfilled for the salvation of humanity and for the glory of the Creator.

A united effort by theologians in this regard, inspired by a convinced adherence to the Magisterium, which is the one authentic guide for the People of God, is particularly urgent for reasons that include the close link between Catholic teaching on this matter and the view of the human person that the Church proposes: doubt or error in the field of marriage or the family involves obscuring to a serious extent the integral truth about the human person in a cultural situation that is already so often confused and contradictory. In fulfillment of their specific role, theologians are called upon to provide enlightenment and a deeper understanding, and their contribution is of incomparable value and represents a unique and highly meritorious service to the family and humanity.

In an integral vision of the human person and of his or her vocation

32. In the context of a culture which seriously distorts or entirely misinterprets the true meaning of human sexuality, because it separates it from its essential reference to the person, the Church more urgently feels how irreplaceable is her mission of presenting sexuality as a value and task of the whole person, created male and female in the image of God.

In this perspective the Second Vatican Council clearly affirmed that "when there is a question of harmonizing conjugal love with the responsible transmission of life, the moral aspect of any procedure does not depend solely on sincere intentions or on an evaluation of motives. It must be determined by *objective standards*. These, *based on the nature of the human person and his or her acts*, preserve the full sense of mutual self-giving and human procreation in the context of true love. Such a goal cannot be achieved unless the virtue of conjugal chastity is sincerely practiced."[86]

It is precisely by moving from "an integral vision of man and of his vocation, not only his natural and earthly, but also his supernatural and eternal vocation,"[87] that Paul VI affirmed that the teaching of the Church "is founded upon the inseparable connection, willed by God and unable to be broken by man on his own initiative, between the two meanings of the conjugal act: the unitive meaning and the procreative meaning."[88] And he concluded by re-emphasizing that there must be excluded as intrinsically immoral "every action which, either in anticipation of the conjugal act, or in its accomplishment, or in the development of its natural consequences, proposes, whether as an end or as a means, to render procreation impossible."[89]

When couples, by means of recourse to contraception, separate these two meanings that God the Creator has inscribed in the being of man and woman and in the dynamism of their sexual communion, they act as "arbiters" of the divine plan and they "manipulate" and degrade human sexuality—and with it themselves and their married partner—by altering its value of "total" self-giving. Thus the innate language that expresses the total reciprocal self-giving of husband and wife is overlaid, through contraception, by an objectively contradictory language, namely, that of not giving oneself totally to the other. This leads not only to a positive refusal to be open to life but also to a falsification of the inner truth of conjugal love, which is called upon to give itself in personal totality.

When, instead, by means of recourse to periods of infertility, the couple respects the inseparable connection between the unitive and procreative meanings of human sexuality, they are acting as "ministers" of God's plan and they "benefit from" their sexuality according to the original dynamism of "total" self-giving, without manipulation or alteration.[90]

In the light of the experience of many couples and of the data provided by the different human sciences, theological reflection is able to perceive and is called to study further *the difference, both anthropological and moral*, between contraception and recourse to the rhythm of the cycle: it is a difference which is much wider and deeper than is usually thought, one which involves in the final analysis two irreconcilable concepts of the human person and of human sexuality. The choice of the natural rhythms involves accepting the cycle of the person, that is the woman, and thereby accepting dialogue, reciprocal respect, shared responsibility, and self-control. To accept the cycle and to enter into dialogue means to recognize both the spiritual and corporal character of conjugal communion and to live personal love with its requirement of fidelity. In this context the couple comes to experience how conjugal communion is enriched with those values of tenderness and affection which constitute the inner soul of human sexuality, in its physical dimension also. In this way sexuality is respected and promoted in its truly and fully human dimension, and is never "used" as an "object" that, by breaking the personal unity of soul and body, strikes at God's creation itself at the level of the deepest interaction of nature and person.

The Church as Teacher and Mother for couples in difficulty

33. In the field of conjugal morality the Church is Teacher and Mother and acts as such.

As Teacher, she never tires of proclaiming the moral norm that must guide the responsible transmission of life. The Church is in no way the author or the arbiter of this norm. In obedience to the truth which is Christ, whose image is reflected in the nature and dignity of the human person, the Church interprets the moral norm and proposes it to all people of good will, without concealing its demands of radicalness and perfection.

As Mother, the Church is close to the many married couples who find themselves in difficulty over this important point of the moral life: she knows well their situation, which is often very arduous and at times truly tormented by difficulties of every kind, not only individual difficulties but social ones as well; she knows that many couples encounter difficulties not only in the concrete fulfillment of the moral norm but even in understanding its inherent values.

But it is one and the same Church that is both Teacher and Mother. And so the Church never ceases to exhort and encourage all to resolve whatever conjugal difficulties may arise without ever falsifying or compromising the truth: she is convinced that there can be no true contradiction between the divine law on transmitting life and that on fostering authentic married love.[91] Accordingly, the concrete pedagogy of the Church must always remain linked with her doctrine and never be separated from it. With the same conviction as my predecessor, I therefore repeat: "To diminish in no way the saving teaching of Christ constitutes an eminent form of charity for souls."[92]

On the other hand, authentic ecclesial pedagogy displays its realism and wisdom only by making a tenacious and courageous effort to create and uphold all the human conditions—psychological, moral, and spiritual—indispensable for understanding and living the moral value and norm.

There is no doubt that these conditions must include persistence and patience, humility and strength of mind, filial trust in God and in his grace, and frequent recourse to prayer and to the sacraments of the Eucharist and of Reconciliation.[93] Thus strengthened, Christian husbands and wives will be able to keep alive their awareness of the unique influence that the grace of the sacrament of Marriage has on every aspect of married life, including therefore their sexuality: the gift of the Spirit, accepted and responded to by husband and wife, helps them to live their human sexuality in accordance with God's plan and as a sign of the unitive and fruitful love of Christ for his Church.

But the necessary conditions also include knowledge of the bodily aspect and the body's rhythms of fertility. Accordingly, every effort must be made to render such knowledge accessible to all married people and also to young adults before marriage, through clear, timely, and serious instruction and education given by married couples, doctors, and experts. Knowledge must then lead to education in self-control: hence the absolute necessity for the virtue of chastity and for permanent education in it. In the Christian view, chastity by no means signifies rejection of human sexuality or lack of esteem for it: rather it signifies spiritual energy capable of defending love from the perils of selfishness and aggressiveness, and able to advance it toward its full realization.

With deeply wise and loving intuition, Paul VI was only voicing the experience of many married couples when he wrote in his encyclical: "To dominate instinct by means of one's reason and free will undoubtedly requires ascetical practices, so that the affective manifestations of conjugal life may observe the correct order, in particular with regard to the observance of periodic continence. Yet this discipline which is proper to the purity of married couples, far from harming conjugal love, rather confers on it a higher human value. It demands continual effort, yet, thanks to its beneficent influence, husband and wife fully develop their personalities, being enriched with spiritual values. Such discipline bestows upon family life fruits of serenity and peace, and facilitates the solution of other problems; it favors attention for one's partner, helps both parties to drive out selfishness, the enemy of true love, and deepens their sense of responsibility. By its means, parents acquire the capacity of having a deeper and more efficacious influence in the education of their offspring."[94]

The moral progress of married people

34. It is always very important to have a right notion of the moral order, its values and its norms; and the importance is all the greater when the difficulties in the way of respecting them become more numerous and serious.

Since the moral order reveals and sets forth the plan of God the Creator, for this very reason it cannot be something that harms man, something impersonal. On the contrary, by responding to the deepest demands of the human being created by God, it places itself at the service of that person's full humanity with the delicate and binding love whereby God himself inspires, sustains, and guides every creature toward its happiness.

But man, who has been called to live God's wise and loving design in a responsible manner, is a historical being who day by day builds himself up through his many free decisions; and so he knows, loves, and accomplishes moral good by stages of growth.

Married people too are called upon to progress unceasingly in their moral life, with the support of a sincere and active desire to gain ever better knowledge of the values enshrined in and fostered by the law of God. They must also be supported by an upright and generous willingness to embody these values in their concrete decisions. They cannot, however, look on the law as merely an ideal to be achieved in the future: they must consider it as a command of Christ the Lord to overcome difficulties with constancy. "And so what is known as 'the law of gradualness' or step-by-step advance cannot be identified with 'gradualness of the law,' as if there were different degrees or forms of precept in God's law for different individuals and situations. In God's plan, all husbands and wives are called in marriage to holiness, and this lofty vocation is fulfilled to the extent that the human person is able to respond to God's command with serene confidence in God's grace and in his or her own will."[95] On the same lines, it is part of the Church's pedagogy that husbands and wives should first of all recognize clearly the teaching of *Humanae Vitae* as indicating the norm for the exercise of their sexuality, and that they should endeavor to establish the conditions necessary for observing that norm.

As the Synod noted, this pedagogy embraces the whole of married life. Accordingly, the function of transmitting life must be integrated into the overall mission of Christian life as a whole, which without the cross cannot reach the resurrection. In such a context it is understandable that sacrifice cannot be removed from family life, but must in fact be wholeheartedly accepted if the love between husband and wife is to be deepened and become a source of intimate joy.

This shared progress demands reflection, instruction, and suitable education on the part of the priests, religious, and lay people engaged in family pastoral work: they will all be able to assist married people in their human and spiritual progress, a progress that demands awareness of sin, a sincere commitment to observe the moral law, and the ministry of reconciliation. It must also be kept in mind that conjugal intimacy involves the wills of two persons, who are however called to harmonize their mentality and behavior: this requires much patience, understanding, and time. Uniquely important in this field is unity of moral and pastoral judgment by priests, a unity that must be carefully sought and ensured, in order that the faithful may not have to suffer anxiety of conscience.[96]

It will be easier for married people to make progress if, with respect for the Church's teaching and with trust in the grace of Christ, and with the help and support of the pastors of souls and the entire ecclesial community, they are able to discover and experience the liberating and inspiring value of the authentic love that is offered by the Gospel and set before us by the Lord's commandment.

Instilling conviction and offering practical help

35. With regard to the question of lawful birth regulation, the ecclesial community at the present time must take on the task of instilling conviction and offering practical help to those who wish to live out their parenthood in a truly responsible way.

In this matter, while the Church notes with satisfaction the results achieved by scientific research aimed at a more precise knowledge of the rhythms of women's fertility, and while it encourages a more decisive and wide-ranging extension of that research, it cannot fail to call with renewed vigor on the responsibility of all—doctors, experts, marriage counselors, teachers and married couples—who can actually help married people to live their love with respect for the structure and finalities of the conjugal act which expresses that love. This implies a broader, more decisive, and more systematic effort to make the natural methods of regulating fertility known, respected, and applied.[97]

A very valuable witness can and should be given by those husbands and wives who through the joint exercise of periodic continence have reached a more mature personal responsibility with regard to love and life. As Paul VI wrote: "To them the Lord entrusts the task of making visible to people the holiness and sweetness of the law which unites the mutual love of husband and wife with their cooperation with the love of God, the author of human life."[98]

2. Education

The right and duty of parents regarding education

36. The task of giving education is rooted in the primary vocation of married couples to participate in God's creative activity: by begetting in love and for love a new person who has within himself or herself the vocation to growth and development, parents by that very fact take on the task of helping that person effectively to live a fully human life. As the Second Vatican Council recalled, "since parents have conferred life on their children, they have a most solemn obligation to educate their offspring. Hence, parents must be acknowledged as the first and foremost educators of their children. Their role as educators is so decisive that scarcely anything can compensate for their failure in it. For it devolves on parents to create a family atmosphere so animated with love and reverence for God and others that a well-rounded personal and social development will be fostered among the children. Hence, the family is the first school of those social virtues which every society needs."[99]

The right and duty of parents to give education is essential, since it is connected with the transmission of human life; it is *original and primary* with regard to the educational role of others, on account of the uniqueness of the loving relationship between parents and children; and it is *irreplaceable and inalienable*, and therefore incapable of being entirely delegated to others or usurped by others.

In addition to these characteristics, it cannot be forgotten that the most basic element, so basic that it qualifies the educational role of parents, is *parental love*, which finds fulfillment in the task of education as it completes and perfects its service of life: as well as being a *source*, the parents' love is also the *animating principle* and therefore the *norm* inspiring and guiding all concrete educational activity, enriching it with the values of kindness, constancy, goodness, service, disinterestedness, and self-sacrifice that are the most precious fruit of love.

Educating in the essential values of human life

37. Even amid the difficulties of the work of education, difficulties which are often greater today, parents must trustingly and courageously train their children in the essential values of human life. Children must grow up with a correct attitude of freedom with regard to material goods, by adopting a simple and austere lifestyle and being fully convinced that "man is more precious for what he is than for what he has."[100]

In a society shaken and split by tensions and conflicts caused by the violent clash of various kinds of individualism and selfishness, children must be enriched not only with a sense of true justice, which alone leads to respect for the personal dignity of each individual, but also and more powerfully by a sense of true love, understood as sincere solicitude and disinterested service with regard to others, especially the poorest and those in most need. The family is the first and fundamental school of social living: as a community of love, it finds in self-giving the law that guides it and makes it grow. The self-giving that inspires the love of husband and wife for each other is the model and norm for the self-giving that must be practiced in the relationships between brothers and sisters and the different generations living together in the family. And the communion and sharing that are part of everyday life in the home at times of joy and at times of difficulty are the most concrete and effective pedagogy for the active, responsible, and fruitful inclusion of the children in the wider horizon of society.

Education in love as self-giving is also the indispensable premise for parents called to give their children a clear and delicate *sex education*. Faced with a culture that largely reduces human sexuality to the level of something commonplace, since it interprets and lives it in a reductive and impoverished way by linking it solely with the body and with selfish pleasure, the educational service of parents must aim firmly at a training in the area of sex that is truly and fully personal: for sexuality is an enrichment of the whole person—body, emotions, and soul—and it manifests its inmost meaning in leading the person to the gift of self in love.

Sex education, which is a basic right and duty of parents, must always be carried out under their attentive guidance, whether at home or in educational centers chosen and controlled by them. In this regard, the Church reaffirms the law of subsidiarity, which the school is bound to observe when it cooperates in sex education, by entering into the same spirit that animates the parents.

In this context *education for chastity* is absolutely essential, for it is a virtue that develops a person's authentic maturity and makes him or her capable of respecting and fostering the "nuptial meaning" of the body. Indeed Christian parents, discerning the signs of God's call, will devote special attention and care to education in virginity or celibacy as the supreme form of that self-giving that constitutes the very meaning of human sexuality.

In view of the close links between the sexual dimension of the person and his or her ethical values, education must bring the children to a knowledge of and respect for the moral norms as the necessary and highly valuable guarantee for responsible personal growth in human sexuality.

For this reason the Church is firmly opposed to an often widespread form of imparting sex information dissociated from moral principles. That would merely be an introduction to the experience of pleasure and a stimulus leading to the loss of serenity—while still in the years of innocence—by opening the way to vice.

The mission to educate and the sacrament of Marriage

38. For Christian parents the mission to educate, a mission rooted, as we have said, in their participation in God's creating activity, has a new specific source in the sacrament of Marriage, which consecrates them for the strictly Christian education of their children: that is to say, it calls upon them to share in the very authority and love of God the Father and

Christ the Shepherd, and in the motherly love of the Church, and it enriches them with wisdom, counsel, fortitude, and all the other gifts of the Holy Spirit in order to help the children in their growth as human beings and as Christians.

The sacrament of Marriage gives to the educational role the dignity and vocation of being really and truly a "ministry" of the Church at the service of the building up of her members. So great and splendid is the educational ministry of Christian parents that Saint Thomas has no hesitation in comparing it with the ministry of priests: "Some only propagate and guard spiritual life by a spiritual ministry: this is the role of the sacrament of Orders; others do this for both corporal and spiritual life, and this is brought about by the sacrament of Marriage, by which a man and a woman join in order to beget offspring and bring them up to worship God."[101]

A vivid and attentive awareness of the mission that they have received with the sacrament of Marriage will help Christian parents to place themselves at the service of their children's education with great serenity and trustfulness, and also with a sense of responsibility before God, who calls them and gives them the mission of building up the Church in their children. Thus in the case of baptized people, the family, called together by word and sacrament as the Church of the home, is both teacher and mother, the same as the worldwide Church.

First experience of the Church

39. The mission to educate demands that Christian parents should present to their children all the topics that are

necessary for the gradual maturing of their personality from a Christian and ecclesial point of view. They will therefore follow the educational lines mentioned above, taking care to show their children the depths of significance to which the faith and love of Jesus Christ can lead. Furthermore, their awareness that the Lord is entrusting to them the growth of a child of God, a brother or sister of Christ, a temple of the Holy Spirit, a member of the Church, will support Christian parents in their task of strengthening the gift of divine grace in their children's souls.

The Second Vatican Council describes the content of Christian education as follows: "Such an education does not merely strive to foster maturity . . . in the human person. Rather, its principal aims are these: that as baptized persons are gradually introduced into a knowledge of the mystery of salvation, they may daily grow more conscious of the gift of faith which they have received; that they may learn to adore God the Father in spirit and in truth (cf. Jn 4:23), especially through liturgical worship; that they may be trained to conduct their personal life in true righteousness and holiness, according to their new nature (Eph 4:22–24), and thus grow to maturity, to the stature of the fullness of Christ (cf. Eph 4:13), and devote themselves to the upbuilding of the Mystical Body. Moreover, aware of their calling, they should grow accustomed to giving witness to the hope that is in them (cf. 1 Pt 3:15), and to promoting the Christian transformation of the world."[102]

The Synod too, taking up and developing the indications of the Council, presented the educational mission of the

Christian family as a true ministry through which the Gospel is transmitted and radiated, so that family life itself becomes an itinerary of faith and in some way a Christian initiation and a school of following Christ. Within a family that is aware of this gift, as Paul VI wrote, "all the members evangelize and are evangelized."[103]

By virtue of their ministry of educating, parents are, through the witness of their lives, the first heralds of the Gospel for their children. Furthermore, by praying with their children, by reading the word of God with them and by introducing them deeply through Christian initiation into the Body of Christ—both the Eucharistic and the ecclesial Body—they become fully parents, in that they are begetters not only of bodily life but also of the life that through the Spirit's renewal flows from the cross and resurrection of Christ.

In order that Christian parents may worthily carry out their ministry of educating, the Synod Fathers expressed the hope that a suitable *catechism for families* would be prepared, one that would be clear, brief, and easily assimilated by all. The episcopal conferences were warmly invited to contribute to producing this catechism.

Relations with other educating agents

40. The family is the primary but not the only and exclusive educating community. Man's community aspect itself—both civil and ecclesial—demands and leads to a broader and more articulated activity resulting from well-

ordered collaboration between the various agents of education. All these agents are necessary, even though each can and should play its part in accordance with the special competence and contribution proper to itself.[104]

The educational role of the Christian family therefore has a very important place in organic pastoral work. This involves a new form of cooperation between parents and Christian communities, and between the various educational groups and pastors. In this sense, the renewal of the Catholic school must give special attention both to the parents of the pupils and to the formation of a perfect educating community.

The right of parents to choose an education in conformity with their religious faith must be absolutely guaranteed.

The State and the Church have the obligation to give families all possible aid to enable them to perform their educational role properly. Therefore both the Church and the State must create and foster the institutions and activities that families justly demand, and the aid must be in proportion to the families' needs. However, those in society who are in charge of schools must never forget that the parents have been appointed by God himself as the first and principal educators of their children and that their right is completely inalienable.

But corresponding to their right, parents have a serious duty to commit themselves totally to a cordial and active relationship with the teachers and the school authorities.

If ideologies opposed to the Christian faith are taught in the schools, the family must join with other families, if possible through family associations, and with all its strength and with wisdom help the young not to depart from the faith. In this case the family needs special assistance from pastors of souls, who must never forget that parents have the inviolable right to entrust their children to the ecclesial community.

Manifold service to life

41. Fruitful married love expresses itself in serving life in many ways. Of these ways, begetting and educating children are the most immediate, specific, and irreplaceable. In fact, every act of true love toward a human being bears witness to and perfects the spiritual fecundity of the family, since it is an act of obedience to the deep inner dynamism of love as self-giving to others.

For everyone this perspective is full of value and commitment, and it can be an inspiration in particular for couples who experience physical sterility.

Christian families, recognizing with faith all human beings as children of the same heavenly Father, will respond generously to the children of other families, giving them support and love not as outsiders but as members of the one family of God's children. Christian parents will thus be able to spread their love beyond the bonds of flesh and blood, nourishing the links that are rooted in the spirit and that develop through concrete service to the children of other families, who are often without even the barest necessities.

Christian families will be able to show greater readiness to adopt and foster children who have lost their parents or have been abandoned by them. Rediscovering the warmth of affection of a family, these children will be able to experience God's loving and provident fatherhood witnessed to by Christian parents, and they will thus be able to grow up with serenity and confidence in life. At the same time the whole family will be enriched with the spiritual values of a wider fraternity. Family fecundity must have an unceasing "creativity," a marvelous fruit of the Spirit of God, who opens the eyes of the heart to discover the new needs and sufferings of our society and gives courage for accepting them and responding to them. A vast field of activity lies open to families: today, even more preoccupying than child abandonment is the phenomenon of social and cultural exclusion, which seriously affects the elderly, the sick, the disabled, drug addicts, ex-prisoners, etc.

This broadens enormously the horizons of the parenthood of Christian families: these and many other urgent needs of our time are a challenge to their spiritually fruitful love. With families and through them, the Lord Jesus continues to "have compassion" on the multitudes.

Ponder

The Church's teaching on responsible parenthood is one of its doctrines least understood by the modern world. The skyrocketing costs of educating children in a technological society, the new public roles of women, and fears about an expanding global population have caused many people to reject the biblical affirmation of children as a blessing and instead to view them as a burden. The development of more effective contraception fueled the sexual revolution, which effectively severed the cultural ties that had existed between marriage, sex, and children. This massive shift in attitudes and behaviors has increasingly led many people to view human fertility as a disease rather than a gift. Saint John Paul II described these developments as "an anti-life mentality" (*FC* no 30). Later he described them as part of a larger "culture of death," closely linked with other attacks on human life, such as abortion and euthanasia.[*]

The Church too was rocked by controversy over the issue of birth control. In his 1968 encyclical *Humanae Vitae*, Pope Paul VI made a prophetic defense of the gift of life and reaffirmed the distinction between natural versus contraceptive means of family planning. But this teaching was subjected to a firestorm of criticism—even within the Church. Its defenders also

[*] See *Evangelium Vitae*, nos. 18–24.

struggled to respond to questions as to how oral contraception could be said to violate the natural law and how to understand the teaching concerning: "the inseparable connection . . . between the unitive significance and the procreative significance, which are both inherent to the marriage act."*

In *Familiaris Consortio* and in his catecheses on the body, John Paul II offered clear and comprehensive responses to such questions. If the conjugal act speaks a language of total self-giving between husband and wife, then contraception overlays this with "an objectively contradictory language," a language of withholding and refusal (*FC* no. 32). Husbands and wives therefore "use" one another rather than love one another when they employ contraception. This is because the fertility that is rejected or withheld is not merely a superficial or biological dimension of the person, but an integral part of the man or woman. Natural means of birth regulation, on the other hand, see this fertility as an integral part of the person and the gift of self. Contraception and natural means of family planning, therefore, ultimately rest on "two irreconcilable concepts of the human person and human sexuality" (*FC* no 32). Finally, natural means are not just alternative "methods" of avoiding pregnancy, but are practices that shape the character of the couple, enabling them to grow in self-control and mutual love in their life together.

---

* Pope Paul VI, Encyclical Letter *Humanae Vitae*, no. 12. The citation is from http://www.vatican.va/holy_father/paul_vi/encyclicals/documents/hf_p-vi_enc_25071968_humanae-vitae_en.html (accessed 9/15/14).

At the same time, John Paul II also showed himself to be a true pastor. He was aware of the struggles married couples face in living this teaching, and the need for the Church as a mother to meet them with love, encouragement, and mercy. The Church also supports parents in their educational tasks and other ways in which families serve life, such as through adoption and outreach to the vulnerable outside of their home.

1. Of all the healthy functions of the human body, why is it that in the twenty-first century only human fertility is treated as a disease to be suppressed through chemicals or surgery (which themselves are often harmful to the physical well-being of those who use them)?

2. Do you see children as a gift and blessing? Why? What factors have shaped your view?

3. In his encyclical *Evangelium Vitae* Pope John Paul II teaches that: "despite their differences of nature and moral gravity, contraception and abortion are often closely connected, as fruits of the same tree" (no. 13). How would you explain this connection?

4. What are some ways that families serve life other than caring for and educating their own (natural or adopted) children? How can the Church better affirm and support these efforts?

Pray

Read the story of Hannah in 1 Samuel 1:1–2:11. Spend time prayerfully reflecting on the following questions:

1. In the face of her infertility, how does Hannah respond to her desire for a child?

2. How does she respond to God's answer to her heart's desire?

3. Saint John Chrysostom held up Hannah as a model for Christian parents in his day because she put the spiritual well-being of her child ahead of her own happiness. How did she do this?

4. Now read and reflect on Mary's song of praise (the Magnificat) in Luke 1:46–56. What parallels do you see between it and Hannah's hymn in 1 Samuel 2:1–10? What do these holy women teach you about trust in God? About children? About how God uses families to bring about his plan of salvation?

   Write down the insights that you receive through your prayer and reflection.

ACT

Make a list of all the couples you know who have shared with you that they are struggling with the cross of infertility. Pray for them daily in the coming week. Encourage others in your family and parish also to pray for infertile couples.

III. Participating in the Development of Society

The family as the first and vital cell of society

42. "Since the Creator of all things has established the conjugal partnership as the beginning and basis of human society," the family is "the first and vital cell of society."[105]

The family has vital and organic links with society, since it is its foundation and nourishes it continually through its role of service to life: it is from the family that citizens come to birth and it is within the family that they find the first school of the social virtues that are the animating principle of the existence and development of society itself.

Thus, far from being closed in on itself, the family is by nature and vocation open to other families and to society, and undertakes its social role.

Family life as an experience of communion and sharing

43. The very experience of communion and sharing that should characterize the family's daily life represents its first and fundamental contribution to society.

The relationships between the members of the family community are inspired and guided by the law of "free giving." By respecting and fostering personal dignity in each and every one as the only basis for value, this free giving takes the form of heartfelt acceptance, encounter and dialogue, disinterested availability, generous service, and deep solidarity.

Thus the fostering of authentic and mature communion between persons within the family is the first and irreplaceable school of social life, and example and stimulus for the broader community relationships marked by respect, justice, dialogue, and love.

The family is thus, as the Synod Fathers recalled, the place of origin and the most effective means for humanizing and personalizing society: it makes an original contribution in depth to building up the world, by making possible a life that is properly speaking human, in particular by guarding and transmitting virtues and "values." As the Second Vatican Council states, in the family "the various generations come together and help one another to grow wiser and to harmonize personal rights with the other requirements of social living."[106]

Consequently, faced with a society that is running the risk of becoming more and more depersonalized and standardized and therefore inhuman and dehumanizing, with the negative results of many forms of escapism—such as alcoholism, drugs, and even terrorism—the family possesses and continues still to release formidable energies capable of taking man out of his anonymity, keeping him conscious of his personal dignity, enriching him with deep humanity, and actively placing him, in his uniqueness and unrepeatability, within the fabric of society.

The social and political role

44. The social role of the family certainly cannot stop short at procreation and education, even if this constitutes its primary and irreplaceable form of expression.

Families, therefore, either singly or in association, can and should devote themselves to manifold social service activities, especially in favor of the poor, or at any rate for the benefit of all people and situations that cannot be reached by the public authorities' welfare organization.

The social contribution of the family has an original character of its own, one that should be given greater recognition and more decisive encouragement, especially as the children grow up, and actually involving all its members as much as possible.[107]

In particular, note must be taken of the ever greater importance in our society of hospitality in all its forms, from opening the door of one's home and still more of one's heart to the pleas of one's brothers and sisters, to concrete efforts to ensure that every family has its own home, as the natural environment that preserves it and makes it grow. In a special way the Christian family is called upon to listen to the Apostle's recommendation: "Practice hospitality,"[108] and, therefore, imitating Christ's example and sharing in his love, to welcome the brother or sister in need: "Whoever gives to one of these little ones even a cup of cold water because he is a disciple, truly, I say to you, he shall not lose his reward."[109]

The social role of families is called upon to find expression also in the form of *political intervention*: families should be the first to take steps to see that the laws and institutions of the State not only do not offend but also support and positively defend the rights and duties of the family. Along these lines, families should grow in awareness of being "protagonists" of what is known as "family politics" and assume responsibility for transforming society; otherwise families will be the first victims of the evils that they have done no more than note with indifference. The Second Vatican Council's appeal to go beyond an individualistic ethic therefore also holds good for the family as such.[110]

Society at the service of the family

45. Just as the intimate connection between the family and society demands that the family be open to and participate in society and its development, so also it requires that society should never fail in its fundamental task of respecting and fostering the family.

The family and society have complementary functions in defending and fostering the good of each and every human being. But society—more specifically the State—must recognize that "the family is a society in its own original right"[111] and so society is under a grave obligation in its relations with the family to adhere to the principle of subsidiarity.

By virtue of this principle, the State cannot and must not take away from families the functions that they can just as well perform on their own or in free associations; instead it must positively favor and encourage as far as possible responsible initiative by families. In the conviction that the good of the family is an indispensable and essential value of the civil community, the public authorities must do everything possible to ensure that families have all those aids—economic, social, educational, political, and cultural assistance—that they need in order to face all their responsibilities in a human way.

The charter of family rights

46. The ideal of mutual support and development between the family and society is often very seriously in conflict with the reality of their separation and even opposition.

In fact, as was repeatedly denounced by the Synod, the situation experienced by many families in various countries is highly problematical, if not entirely negative: institutions and laws unjustly ignore the inviolable rights of the family and of the human person; and society, far from putting itself at the service of the family, attacks it violently in its values and fundamental requirements. Thus the family, which in God's plan is the basic cell of society and a subject of rights and duties before the State or any other community, finds itself the victim of society, of the delays and slowness with which it acts, and even of its blatant injustice.

For this reason, the Church openly and strongly defends the rights of the family against the intolerable usurpations of society and the State. In particular, the Synod Fathers mentioned the following rights of the family:

— the right to exist and progress as a family, that is to say, the right of every human being, even if he or she is poor, to found a family and to have adequate means to support it;

— the right to exercise its responsibility regarding the transmission of life and to educate children;

— the right to the intimacy of conjugal and family life;

— the right to the stability of the bond and of the institution of marriage;

— the right to believe in and profess one's faith and to propagate it;

— the right to bring up children in accordance with the family's own traditions and religious and cultural values, with the necessary instruments, means, and institutions;

— the right, especially of the poor and the sick, to obtain physical, social, political, and economic security;

— the right to housing suitable for living family life in a proper way;

— the right to expression and to representation, either directly or through associations, before the economic, social, and cultural public authorities and lower authorities;

— the right to form associations with other families and institutions, in order to fulfill the family's role suitably and expeditiously;

— the right to protect minors by adequate institutions and legislation from harmful drugs, pornography, alcoholism, etc.;

— the right to wholesome recreation of a kind that also fosters family values;

— the right of the elderly to a worthy life and a worthy death;

— the right to emigrate as a family in search of a better life.[112]

Acceding to the Synod's explicit request, the Holy See will give prompt attention to studying these suggestions in depth and to the preparation of a Charter of Rights of the Family, to be presented to the quarters and authorities concerned.

The Christian family's grace and responsibility

47. The social role that belongs to every family pertains by a new and original right to the Christian family, which is based on the sacrament of Marriage. By taking up the human reality of the love between husband and wife in all its implications, the sacrament gives to Christian couples and parents a power and a commitment to live their vocation as lay people and therefore to "seek the kingdom of God by engaging in temporal affairs and by ordering them according to the plan of God."[113]

The social and political role is included in the kingly mission of service in which Christian couples share by virtue of the sacrament of Marriage, and they receive both a command which they cannot ignore and a grace which sustains and stimulates them.

The Christian family is thus called upon to offer everyone a witness of generous and disinterested dedication to social matters, through a "preferential option" for the poor and disadvantaged. Therefore, advancing in its following of the Lord by special love for all the poor, it must have special concern for the hungry, the poor, the old, the sick, drug victims, and those who have no family.

For a new international order

48. In view of the worldwide dimension of various social questions nowadays, the family has seen its role with regard to the development of society extended in a completely new way: it now also involves cooperating for a new international order, since it is only in worldwide solidarity that the enormous and dramatic issues of world justice, the freedom of peoples, and the peace of humanity can be dealt with and solved.

The spiritual communion between Christian families, rooted in a common faith and hope and given life by love, constitutes an inner energy that generates, spreads, and develops justice, reconciliation, fraternity, and peace among human beings. Insofar as it is a "small-scale Church," the Christian family is called upon, like the "large-scale Church," to be a sign of unity for the world and in this way to exercise its prophetic role by bearing witness to the Kingdom and peace of Christ, toward which the whole world is journeying.

Christian families can do this through their educational activity—that is to say by presenting to their children a model of life based on the values of truth, freedom, justice, and love—both through active and responsible involvement in the authentically human growth of society and its institutions, and by supporting in various ways the associations specifically devoted to international issues.

Ponder

The mission of the family does not stop at the walls of its own house. The Church understands that families have an indispensable social role, serving as "the first and vital cell of society" (*FC* no. 42). *

The family is the place where persons discover their own identity and humanity in relationships of love, care, and giving. It therefore serves as a place of socialization and moral formation. It shapes the capacities of its members to relate to others justly and to build relationships of justice, solidarity, and friendship outside of the home—"the first and irreplaceable school of social life," as John Paul II puts it (*FC* no. 43). Christian families imbue this process of formation with the light of the Gospel, capacitating their members to live in the communion of truth and love.

Families do not just give birth to and raise future members of society. Families are called to make a difference in their communities by caring for the poor and practicing hospitality in the name of Christ. They also need to be engaged politically in their communities and nations, serving as " 'protagonists' of what is known as 'family politics' and assum[ing] responsibility for transforming society" (*FC* no. 44). This is in keeping

---

* Pope John Paul II is here quoting a phrase used by the Second Vatican Council in its *Decree on the Apostolate of the Laity* (*Apostolicam Actuositatem*), no. 11.

with the Second Vatican Council's vision of the laity's role to transform the world around them through their lives, work, and witness. The Council taught: "They exercise the apostolate in fact by their activity directed to the evangelization and sanctification of men and to the penetrating and perfecting of the temporal order through the spirit of the Gospel."*

The family has profound importance as the first and most fundamental place of human formation. So the State has an important responsibility to protect the family from economic, cultural, and political forces that would weaken or attack it. Instead, the State should pursue policies that support the family's autonomy and well-being. In particular, the State's actions toward the family must be governed by the principle of subsidiarity, which states that: "a community of a higher order should not interfere in the internal life of a community of a lower order, depriving the latter of its functions, but rather should support it in case of need and help to co-ordinate its activity with the activities of the rest of society, always with a view to the common good."† Thus parents—not the State—have the primary responsibility for raising their children.

To underscore the important point that the State needs to respect the family, Pope John Paul II enumerates a set of

---

* *Apostolicam Actuositatem*, no. 2. The citation is from http://www.vatican.va/archive/hist_councils/ii_vatican_council/documents/vat-ii_decree_19651118_apostolicam-actuositatem_en.html (assessed 9/14/15).

† Pope John Paul II, Encyclical Letter *Centesimus Annus* (1991), no. 48, cited in the *Catechism of the Catholic Church*, 1883.

fundamental rights of the family that the State must seek to safeguard. These rights were eventually given a fuller elaboration in the Holy See's Charter of the Rights of the Family promulgated in 1983 and directed to the international community.[*]

1. What is the family's role in socializing and forming its members according to Pope John Paul II?

2. In his *Letter to Families* (no. 9) Saint John Paul II speaks of the family as the "genealogy of the person," shaping the identity of the child born into it. At the same time the child is a "gift" and "mystery," a unique and unrepeatable person in the image and likeness of God. How have you been shaped by your family of origin? In what ways do your identity and gifts transcend your family?

3. Why do you think it is important to translate your understanding of the family into your engagement as a voting citizen? How would this affect the way you vote?

4. Why is it crucial to insist that the family, like the human person, has fundamental rights that are not given to it by the State? Do you see any ways in which the government of your country is encroaching on the

---

[*] The document is available at http://www.vatican.va/roman_curia/pontifical_councils/family/documents/rc_pc_family_doc_19831022_family-rights_en.html (accessed 9/14/15).

rights outlined in this document? If so, what response is called for?

Pray

John Paul II draws our attention to Matthew 10:42: "And whoever gives only a cup of cold water to one of these little ones to drink because he is a disciple—amen, I say to you, he will surely not lose his reward" (see *FC* no. 44). The Pope wants to underscore the family's role in providing Christian hospitality to brothers and sisters in need. In this text in Matthew 10, Jesus' identification with needy members of the Christian community anticipates his later identification with the stranger, the naked, the sick, and the imprisoned in the eschatological judgment scene of Matthew 25:31–46. Read this text slowly and prayerfully.

1. Before you begin this reading, consider that neither the "sheep" nor the "goats" recognize Jesus in the vulnerable persons whom they encounter. They see only the needy human beings before them and either care for them or fail to do so. They allow themselves to be moved by love or self-interest. Ask God for the grace to respond in love to those around you.

2. Spend time prayerfully reflecting on Jesus' words to the righteous, "Amen, I say to you, whatever you did for one of these least brothers of mine, you did for me" (Mt 25:40). Ask the Lord to deepen your faith and hope.

3. Imagine yourself standing with your family before Christ the King as he judges the nations. Where are you standing? Imagine Jesus speaking to you. What does he say? How do you respond? Ask the Lord to show you how you and your family might better respond to the vulnerable persons around you and, in doing so, respond to him.

Act

Plan an activity for yourself or your family in which you have the opportunity to serve vulnerable people in your community (e.g., volunteer at a soup kitchen, visit a nursing home, help out at a crisis pregnancy center).

IV. Sharing in the Life and Mission of the Church

The family, within the mystery of the Church

49. Among the fundamental tasks of the Christian family is its ecclesial task: the family is placed at the service of the building up of the Kingdom of God in history by participating in the life and mission of the Church.

In order to understand better the foundations, the contents, and the characteristics of this participation, we must examine the many profound bonds linking the Church and the Christian family and establishing the family as a "Church in miniature" (*Ecclesia domestica*),[114] in such a way that in its own way the family is a living image and historical representation of the mystery of the Church.

It is, above all, the Church as Mother that gives birth to, educates, and builds up the Christian family, by putting into effect in its regard the saving mission which she has received from her Lord. By proclaiming the word of God, the Church reveals to the Christian family its true identity, what it is and should be according to the Lord's plan; by celebrating the sacraments, the Church enriches and strengthens the Christian family with the grace of Christ for its sanctification to the glory of the Father; by the continuous proclamation of the new commandment of love, the Church encourages and guides the Christian family to the service of love, so that it may imitate and relive the same self-giving and sacrificial love that the Lord Jesus has for the entire human race.

In turn, the Christian family is grafted into the mystery of the Church to such a degree as to become a sharer, in its own way, in the saving mission proper to the Church: by virtue of the sacrament, Christian married couples and parents "in their state and way of life have their own special gift among the People of God."[115] For this reason they not only *receive* the love of Christ and become a *saved* community, but they are also called upon to *communicate* Christ's love to their brethren, thus becoming a *saving* community. In this way, while the Christian family is a fruit and sign of the supernatural fecundity of the Church, it stands also as a symbol, witness, and participant of the Church's motherhood.[116]

A specific and original ecclesial role

50. The Christian family is called upon to take part actively and responsibly in the mission of the Church in a way that is original and specific, by placing itself, in what it is and what it does as an "intimate community of life and love," at the service of the Church and of society.

Since the Christian family is a community in which the relationships are renewed by Christ through faith and the sacraments, the family's sharing in the Church's mission should follow a *community pattern*: the spouses together *as a couple*, the parents and children *as a family*, must live their service to the Church and to the world. They must be "of one heart and soul"[117] in faith, through the shared apostolic zeal that animates them, and through their shared commitment to works of service to the ecclesial and civil communities.

The Christian family also builds up the Kingdom of God in history through the everyday realities that concern and distinguish its *state of life*. It is thus in *the love between husband and wife and between the members of the family*—a love lived out in all its extraordinary richness of values and demands: totality, oneness, fidelity, and fruitfulness[118] that the Christian family's participation in the prophetic, priestly, and kingly mission of Jesus Christ and of his Church finds expression and realization. Therefore, love and life constitute the nucleus of the saving mission of the Christian family in the Church and for the Church.

The Second Vatican Council recalls this fact when it writes: "Families will share their spiritual riches generously with other families too. Thus the Christian family, which springs from marriage as a reflection of the loving covenant uniting Christ with the Church, and as a participation in that covenant will manifest to all people the Savior's living presence in the world and the genuine nature of the Church. This the family will do by the mutual love of the spouses, by their generous fruitfulness, their solidarity and faithfulness, and by the loving way in which all the members of the family work together."[119]

Having laid the *foundation* of the participation of the Christian family in the Church's mission, it is now time to illustrate its *substance in reference to Jesus Christ as Prophet, Priest, and King*—three aspects of a single reality—by presenting the Christian family as 1) a believing and evangelizing community, 2) a community in dialogue with God, and 3) a community at the service of man.

1. The Christian family as a believing and evangelizing community

Faith as the discovery and admiring awareness of God's plan for the family

51. As a sharer in the life and mission of the Church, which listens to the word of God with reverence and proclaims it confidently,[120] *the Christian family fulfills its prophetic role by welcoming and announcing the word of God*: it thus becomes more and more each day a believing and evangelizing community.

Christian spouses and parents are required to offer "the obedience of faith."[121] They are called upon to welcome the word of the Lord which reveals to them the marvelous news— the Good News—of their conjugal and family life sanctified and made a source of sanctity by Christ himself. Only in faith can they discover and admire with joyful gratitude the dignity to which God has deigned to raise marriage and the family, making them a sign and meeting place of the loving covenant between God and man, between Jesus Christ and his bride, the Church.

The very preparation for Christian marriage is itself a journey of faith. It is a special opportunity for the engaged to rediscover and deepen the faith received in Baptism and nourished by their Christian upbringing. In this way they come to recognize and freely accept their vocation to follow Christ and to serve the Kingdom of God in the married state.

The celebration of the sacrament of Marriage is the basic moment of the faith of the couple. This sacrament, in essence, is the proclamation in the Church of the Good News concerning married love. It is the word of God that "reveals" and "fulfills" the wise and loving plan of God for the married couple, giving them a mysterious and real share in the very love with which God himself loves humanity. Since the sacramental celebration of marriage is itself a proclamation of the word of God, it must also be a "profession of faith" within and with the Church, as a community of believers, on the part of all those who in different ways participate in its celebration.

This profession of faith demands that it be prolonged in the life of the married couple and of the family. God, who called the couple to marriage, continues to call them in marriage.[122] In and through the events, problems, difficulties, and circumstances of everyday life, God comes to them, revealing and presenting the concrete "demands" of their sharing in the love of Christ for his Church in the particular family, social, and ecclesial situation in which they find themselves.

The discovery of and obedience to the plan of God on the part of the conjugal and family community must take place in "togetherness," through the human experience of love between husband and wife, between parents and children, lived in the Spirit of Christ.

Thus the little domestic church, like the greater Church, needs to be constantly and intensely evangelized: hence its duty regarding permanent education in the faith.

The Christian family's ministry of evangelization

52. To the extent in which the Christian family accepts the Gospel and matures in faith, it becomes an evangelizing

community. Let us listen again to Paul VI: "The family, like the Church, ought to be a place where the Gospel is transmitted and from which the Gospel radiates. In a family which is conscious of this mission, all the members evangelize and are evangelized. The parents not only communicate the Gospel to their children, but from their children they can themselves receive the same Gospel as deeply lived by them. And such a family becomes the evangelizer of many other families, and of the neighborhood of which it forms part."[123]

As the Synod repeated, taking up the appeal which I launched at Puebla, the future of evangelization depends in great part on the church of the home.[124] This apostolic mission of the family is rooted in Baptism and receives from the grace of the sacrament of Marriage new strength to transmit the faith, to sanctify and transform our present society according to God's plan.

Particularly today, the Christian family has a special vocation to witness to the paschal covenant of Christ by constantly radiating the joy of love and the certainty of the hope for which it must give an account: "The Christian family loudly proclaims both the present virtues of the Kingdom of God and the hope of a blessed life to come."[125]

The absolute need for family catechesis emerges with particular force in certain situations that the Church unfortunately experiences in some places: "In places where anti-religious legislation endeavors even to prevent education in the faith, and in places where widespread unbelief or invasive secularism makes real religious growth practically impossible, 'the Church of the home' remains the one place where children and young people can receive an authentic catechesis."[126]

Ecclesial service

53. The ministry of evangelization carried out by Christian parents is original and irreplaceable. It assumes the characteristics typical of family life itself, which should be interwoven with love, simplicity, practicality, and daily witness.[127]

The family must educate the children for life in such a way that each one may fully perform his or her role according to the vocation received from God. Indeed, the family that is open to transcendent values, that serves its brothers and sisters with joy, that fulfills its duties with generous fidelity, and is aware of its daily sharing in the mystery of the glorious cross of Christ, becomes the primary and most excellent seedbed of vocations to a life of consecration to the Kingdom of God.

The parents' ministry of evangelization and catechesis ought to play a part in their children's lives also during adolescence and youth, when the children, as often happens, challenge or even reject the Christian faith received in earlier years. Just as in the Church the work of evangelization can never be separated from the sufferings of the apostle, so in the Christian family parents must face with courage and great interior serenity the difficulties that their ministry of evangelization sometimes encounters in their own children.

It should not be forgotten that the service rendered by Christian spouses and parents to the Gospel is essentially an ecclesial service. It has its place within the context of the whole Church as an evangelized and evangelizing community. Insofar as the ministry of evangelization and catechesis of the church of the home is rooted in and derives from the one mission of the Church and is ordained to the up-building of the one Body of Christ,[128] it must remain in intimate communion and collaborate responsibly with all the other evangelizing and catechetical activities present and at work in the ecclesial community at the diocesan and parochial levels.

To preach the Gospel to the whole creation

54. Evangelization, urged on within by irrepressible missionary zeal, is characterized by a universality without boundaries. It is the response to Christ's explicit and unequivocal command: "Go into all the world and preach the Gospel to the whole creation."[129]

The Christian family's faith and evangelizing mission also possesses this catholic missionary inspiration. The sacrament of Marriage takes up and reproposes the task of defending and spreading the faith, a task that has its roots in Baptism and Confirmation,[130] and makes Christian married couples and parents witnesses of Christ "to the end of the earth,"[131] missionaries, in the true and proper sense, of love and life.

A form of missionary activity can be exercised even within the family. This happens when some member of the family does not have the faith or does not practice it with consistency. In such a case the other members must give him or her a living witness of their own faith in order to encourage and support him or her along the path toward full acceptance of Christ the Savior.[132]

Animated in its own inner life by missionary zeal, the Church of the home is also called to be a luminous sign of the presence of Christ and of his love for those who are "far away," for families who do not yet believe, and for those Christian families who no longer live in accordance with the faith that they once received. The Christian family is called to enlighten "by its example and its witness . . . those who seek the truth."[133]

Just as at the dawn of Christianity Aquila and Priscilla were presented as a missionary couple,[134] so today the Church shows forth her perennial newness and fruitfulness by the presence of Christian couples and families who dedicate at least a part of their lives to working in missionary territories, proclaiming the Gospel and doing service to their fellowman in the love of Jesus Christ.

Christian families offer a special contribution to the missionary cause of the Church by fostering missionary vocations among their sons and daughters[135] and, more generally, "by training their children from childhood to recognize God's love for all people."[136]

2. The Christian family as a community in dialogue with God

The Church's sanctuary in the home

55. The proclamation of the Gospel and its acceptance in faith reach their fullness in the celebration of the sacraments. The Church, which is a believing and evangelizing

community, is also a priestly people invested with the dignity and sharing in the power of Christ the High Priest of the New and Eternal Covenant.[137]

The Christian family too is part of this priestly people which is the Church. By means of the sacrament of Marriage, in which it is rooted and from which it draws its nourishment, the Christian family is continuously vivified by the Lord Jesus and called and engaged by him in a dialogue with God through the sacraments, through the offering of one's life, and through prayer.

This is the *priestly role* which the Christian family can and ought to exercise in intimate communion with the whole Church, through the daily realities of married and family life. In this way the Christian family *is called to be sanctified and to sanctify the ecclesial community and the world.*

Marriage as a sacrament of mutual sanctification and an act of worship

56. The sacrament of Marriage is the specific source and original means of sanctification for Christian married couples and families. It takes up again and makes specific the sanctifying grace of Baptism. By virtue of the mystery of the death and resurrection of Christ, of which the spouses are made part in a new way by marriage, conjugal love is purified and made holy: "This love the Lord has judged worthy of special gifts, healing, perfecting, and exalting gifts of grace and of charity."[138]

The gift of Jesus Christ is not exhausted in the actual celebration of the sacrament of Marriage, but rather accompanies the married couple throughout their lives. This fact is explicitly recalled by the Second Vatican Council when it says that Jesus Christ "abides with them so that, just as he loved the Church and handed himself over on her behalf, the spouses may love each other with perpetual fidelity through mutual self-bestowal. . . . For this reason, Christian spouses have a special sacrament by which they are fortified and receive a kind of consecration in the duties and dignity of their state. By virtue of this sacrament, as spouses fulfill their conjugal and family obligations, they are penetrated with the Spirit of Christ, who fills their whole lives with faith, hope, and charity. Thus they increasingly advance toward their own perfection, as well as toward their mutual sanctification, and hence contribute jointly to the glory of God."[139]

Christian spouses and parents are included in the universal call to sanctity. For them this call is specified by the sacrament they have celebrated and is carried out concretely in the realities proper to their conjugal and family life.[140] This gives rise to the grace and requirement of an authentic and profound *conjugal and family spirituality* that draws its inspiration from the themes of creation, covenant, cross, resurrection, and sign, which were stressed more than once by the Synod.

Christian marriage, like the other sacraments, "whose purpose is to sanctify people, to build up the body of Christ, and finally, to give worship to God,"[141] is in itself a liturgical action glorifying God in Jesus Christ and in the Church. By celebrating it, Christian spouses profess their gratitude to God for the sublime gift bestowed on them of being able to live in their married and family lives the very love of God for people and that of the Lord Jesus for the Church, his bride.

Just as husbands and wives receive from the sacrament the gift and responsibility of translating into daily living the sanctification bestowed on them, so the same sacrament confers on them the grace and moral obligation of transforming their whole lives into a "spiritual sacrifice."[142] What the Council says of the laity applies also to Christian spouses and parents, especially with regard to the earthly and temporal realities that characterize their lives: "As worshippers leading holy lives in every place, the laity consecrate the world itself to God."[143]

Marriage and the Eucharist

57. The Christian family's sanctifying role is grounded in Baptism and has its highest expression in the Eucharist, to which Christian marriage is intimately connected. The Second Vatican Council drew attention to the unique relationship between the Eucharist and marriage by requesting that "marriage normally be celebrated within the Mass."[144] To understand better and live more intensely the graces and responsibilities of Christian marriage and family life, it is altogether necessary to rediscover and strengthen this relationship.

The Eucharist is the very source of Christian marriage. The Eucharistic Sacrifice, in fact, represents Christ's covenant of love with the Church, sealed with his blood on the cross.[145]

In this sacrifice of the new and eternal Covenant, Christian spouses encounter the source from which their own marriage covenant flows, is interiorly structured, and continuously renewed. As a representation of Christ's sacrifice of love for the Church, the Eucharist is a fountain of charity. In the Eucharistic gift of charity the Christian family finds the foundation and soul of its "communion" and its "mission": by partaking in the Eucharistic bread, the different members of the Christian family become one body, which reveals and shares in the wider unity of the Church. Their sharing in the Body of Christ that is "given up" and in his Blood that is "shed" becomes a never-ending source of missionary and apostolic dynamism for the Christian family.

The sacrament of conversion and reconciliation

58. An essential and permanent part of the Christian family's sanctifying role consists in accepting the call to conversion that the Gospel addresses to all Christians, who do not always remain faithful to the "newness" of the Baptism that constitutes them "saints." The Christian family too is sometimes unfaithful to the law of baptismal grace and holiness proclaimed anew in the sacrament of Marriage.

Repentance and mutual pardon within the bosom of the Christian family, so much a part of daily life, receive their specific sacramental expression in Christian Penance. In the Encyclical *Humanae Vitae*, Paul VI wrote of married couples: "And if sin should still keep its hold over them, let them not be discouraged, but rather have recourse with humble perseverance to the mercy of God, which is abundantly poured forth in the sacrament of Penance."[146]

The celebration of this sacrament acquires special significance for family life. While they discover in faith that sin contradicts not only the covenant with God, but also the covenant between husband and wife and the communion of the family, the married couple and the other members of the family are led to an encounter with God, who is "rich in mercy,"[147] who bestows on them his love which is more powerful than sin,[148] and who reconstructs and brings to perfection the marriage covenant and the family communion.

Family prayer

59. The Church prays for the Christian family and educates the family to live in generous accord with the priestly gift and role received from Christ the High Priest. In effect, the baptismal priesthood of the faithful, exercised in the sacrament of Marriage, constitutes the basis of a priestly vocation and mission for the spouses and family by which their daily lives are transformed into "spiritual sacrifices acceptable to God through Jesus Christ."[149] This transformation is achieved not only by celebrating the Eucharist and the other sacraments and through offering themselves to the glory of God, but also through a life of prayer, through prayerful dialogue with the Father, through Jesus Christ, in the Holy Spirit.

Family prayer has its own characteristic qualities. It is prayer offered *in common*, husband and wife together, parents and children together. Communion in prayer is both a consequence of and a requirement for the communion bestowed by the sacraments of Baptism and Matrimony. The words with which the Lord Jesus promises his presence can be applied to the members of the Christian family in a special way: "Again I say to you, if two of you agree on earth about anything they ask, it will be done for them by my Father in heaven. For where two or three are gathered in my name, there am I in the midst of them."[150]

Family prayer has for its very own object *family life itself*, which in all its varying circumstances is seen as a call from God and lived as a filial response to his call. Joys and sorrows, hopes and disappointments, births and birthday celebrations, wedding anniversaries of the parents, departures, separations and homecomings, important and far-reaching decisions, the death of those who are dear, etc.—all of these mark God's loving intervention in the family's history. They should be seen as suitable moments for thanksgiving, for petition, for trusting abandonment of the family into the hands of their common Father in heaven. The dignity and responsibility of the Christian family as the domestic church can be achieved only with God's unceasing aid, which will surely be granted if it is humbly and trustingly petitioned in prayer.

Educators in prayer

60. By reason of their dignity and mission, Christian parents have the specific responsibility of educating their children in prayer, introducing them to gradual discovery of the mystery of God and to personal dialogue with him: "It is

particularly in the Christian family, enriched by the grace and the office of the sacrament of Matrimony, that from the earliest years children should be taught, according to the faith received in Baptism, to have a knowledge of God, to worship him, and to love their neighbor."[151]

The concrete example and living witness of parents is fundamental and irreplaceable in educating their children to pray. Only by praying together with their children can a father and mother—exercising their royal priesthood—penetrate the innermost depths of their children's hearts and leave an impression that the future events in their lives will not be able to efface. Let us again listen to the appeal made by Paul VI to parents: "Mothers, do you teach your children the Christian prayers? Do you prepare them, in conjunction with the priests, for the sacraments that they receive when they are young: Confession, Communion, and Confirmation? Do you encourage them when they are sick to think of Christ suffering, to invoke the aid of the Blessed Virgin and the saints? Do you say the family rosary together? And you, fathers, do you pray with your children, with the whole domestic community, at least sometimes? Your example of honesty in thought and action, joined to some common prayer, is a lesson for life, an act of worship of singular value. In this way you bring peace to your homes: *Pax huic domui*. Remember, it is thus that you build up the Church."[152]

Liturgical prayer and private prayer

61. There exists a deep and vital bond between the prayer of the Church and the prayer of the individual faithful, as has been

clearly reaffirmed by the Second Vatican Council.[153] An important purpose of the prayer of the domestic church is to serve as the natural introduction for the children to the liturgical prayer of the whole Church, both in the sense of preparing for it and of extending it into personal, family, and social life. Hence the need for gradual participation by all the members of the Christian family in the celebration of the Eucharist, especially on Sundays and feast days, and of the other sacraments, particularly the sacraments of Christian initiation of the children. The directives of the Council opened up a new possibility for the Christian family when it listed the family among those groups to whom it recommends the recitation of the Divine Office in common.[154] Likewise, the Christian family will strive to celebrate at home, and in a way suited to the members, the times and feasts of the liturgical year.

As preparation for the worship celebrated in church, and as its prolongation in the home, the Christian family makes use of private prayer, which presents a great variety of forms. While this variety testifies to the extraordinary richness with which the Spirit vivifies Christian prayer, it serves also to meet the various needs and life situations of those who turn to the Lord in prayer. Apart from morning and evening prayers, certain forms of prayer are to be expressly encouraged, following the indications of the Synod Fathers, such as reading and meditating on the word of God, preparation for the reception of the sacraments, devotion and consecration to the Sacred Heart of Jesus, the various forms of veneration of the Blessed Virgin Mary, grace before and after meals, and observance of popular devotions.

While respecting the freedom of the children of God, the Church has always proposed certain practices of piety to the faithful with particular solicitude and insistence. Among these should be mentioned the recitation of the rosary: "We now desire, as a continuation of the thought of our predecessors, to recommend strongly the recitation of the family rosary. . . . There is no doubt that . . . the rosary should be considered as one of the best and most efficacious prayers in common that the Christian family is invited to recite. We like to think, and sincerely hope, that when the family gathering becomes a time of prayer the rosary is a frequent and favored manner of praying."[155] In this way authentic devotion to Mary, which finds expression in sincere love and generous imitation of the Blessed Virgin's interior spiritual attitude, constitutes a special instrument for nourishing loving communion in the family and for developing conjugal and family spirituality. For she who is the Mother of Christ and of the Church is in a special way the Mother of Christian families, of domestic churches.

Prayer and life

62. It should never be forgotten that prayer constitutes an essential part of Christian life, understood in its fullness and centrality. Indeed, prayer is an important part of our very humanity: it is "the first expression of man's inner truth, the first condition for authentic freedom of spirit."[156]

Far from being a form of escapism from everyday commitments, prayer constitutes the strongest incentive for the

Christian family to assume and comply fully with all its responsibilities as the primary and fundamental cell of human society. Thus the Christian family's actual participation in the Church's life and mission is in direct proportion to the fidelity and intensity of the prayer with which it is united with the fruitful vine that is Christ the Lord.[157]

The fruitfulness of the Christian family in its specific service to human advancement, which of itself cannot but lead to the transformation of the world, derives from its living union with Christ, nourished by liturgy, by self-oblation, and by prayer.[158]

3. The Christian family

The new commandment of love

63. The Church, a prophetic, priestly, and kingly people, is endowed with the mission of bringing all human beings to accept the word of God in faith, to celebrate and profess it in the sacraments and in prayer, and to give expression to it in the concrete realities of life in accordance with the gift and new commandment of love.

The law of Christian life is to be found not in a written code, but in the personal action of the Holy Spirit who inspires and guides the Christian. It is the "law of the Spirit of life in Christ Jesus"[159]: "God's love has been poured into our hearts through the Holy Spirit who has been given to us."[160]

This is true also for the Christian couple and family. Their guide and rule of life is the Spirit of Jesus poured into their hearts in the celebration of the sacrament of Matrimony. In continuity with Baptism in water and the Spirit, marriage sets forth anew the evangelical law of love, and with the gift of the Spirit engraves it more profoundly on the hearts of Christian husbands and wives. Their love, purified and saved, is a fruit of the Spirit acting in the hearts of believers and constituting, at the same time, the fundamental commandment of their moral life to be lived in responsible freedom.

Thus, the Christian family is inspired and guided by the new law of the Spirit and, in intimate communion with the Church, the kingly people, it is called to exercise its "service" of love toward God and toward its fellow human beings. Just as Christ exercises his royal power by serving us,[161] so also the Christian finds the authentic meaning of his participation in the kingship of his Lord in sharing his spirit and practice of service to man. "Christ has communicated this power to his disciples that they might be established in royal freedom and that by self-denial and a holy life they might conquer the reign of sin in themselves (cf. Rom 6:12). Further, he has shared this power so that by serving him in their fellow human beings they might through humility and patience lead their brothers and sisters to that King whom to serve is to reign. For the Lord wishes to spread his kingdom by means of the laity also, a kingdom of truth and life, a kingdom of holiness and grace, a kingdom of justice, love, and peace. In this kingdom, creation itself will be delivered out of its slavery to corruption and into the freedom of the glory of the children of God (cf. Rom 8:21)."[162]

To discover the image of God in each brother and sister

64. Inspired and sustained by the new commandment of love, the Christian family welcomes, respects, and serves every human being, considering each one in his or her dignity as a person and as a child of God.

It should be so especially between husband and wife and within the family, through a daily effort to promote a truly personal community, initiated and fostered by an inner communion of love. This way of life should then be extended to the wider circle of the ecclesial community of which the Christian family is a part. Thanks to love within the family, the Church can and ought to take on a more homelike or family dimension, developing a more human and fraternal style of relationships.

Love, too, goes beyond our brothers and sisters of the same faith since "everybody is my brother or sister." In each individual, especially in the poor, the weak, and those who suffer or are unjustly treated, love knows how to discover the face of Christ, and discover a fellow human being to be loved and served.

In order that the family may serve man in a truly evangelical way, the instructions of the Second Vatican Council must be carefully put into practice: "That the exercise of such charity may rise above any deficiencies in fact and even in appearance, certain fundamentals must be observed. Thus, attention is to be paid to the image of God in which our neighbor has been created, and also to Christ the Lord to whom is really offered whatever is given to a needy person."[163]

While building up the Church in love, the Christian family places itself at the service of the human person and the world, really bringing about the "human advancement" whose substance was given in summary form in the Synod's *Message* to families: "Another task for the family is to form persons in love and also to practice love in all its relationships, so that it does not live closed in on itself, but remains open to the community, moved by a sense of justice and concern for others, as well as by a consciousness of its responsibility toward the whole of society."[164]

Ponder

The family does not have only a social mission, it has an ecclesial one. The term "domestic church" has roots in the New Testament, especially in the letters of Saint Paul. The apostle would often send greetings to churches that met in people's homes. Many of the Fathers of the Church (e.g., Saint John Chrysostom, Saint Augustine) encouraged families to live their faith intensely in the midst of their household life. In time, however, because of the growth of monastic and religious life, many people in the Church developed the view that one had to give up marriage and family in order to pursue holiness. Given this history it is significant that Saint John Paul II follows the Second Vatican Council in describing the family as a "domestic" or "miniature" church (*FC* no. 49).* This reopens the way to understand that the universal call to holiness can be lived out in the family. The Council itself had taught that: "in the Church, everyone, whether belonging to the hierarchy, or being cared for by it, is called to holiness."†

---

* See Vatican II's *Dogmatic Constitution on the Church* (*Lumen Gentium*) (1964), no. 11; and *Apostolicam Actuositatem*, no. 11.

† *Lumen Gentium*, no. 39. The citation is from http://www.vatican.va/archive/hist_councils/ii_vatican_council/documents/vat-ii_const_19641121_lumen-gentium_en.html (accessed 9/19/14).

But how do families do this? The Pope responds by pointing us toward the threefold office (*munus*) of Christ as Prophet, Priest, and King. The family acts in its role as prophet *"by welcoming and announcing the word of God"* (*FC* no. 51). This begins with the celebration of marriage itself. In his catecheses on the body, Saint John Paul II describes the wedding vows spoken by the couple as a prophecy of their whole life together.* The family also acts prophetically in speaking the word of God to one another inside and outside the home: "all the members evangelize and are evangelized" (*FC* no. 52).

The priesthood of the family is exercised in the family's life of prayer within the home—both individually and together—and in their participation in the Church's sacramental life. Baptism, Confirmation, Marriage, and Reconciliation all empower the members of the family to live out their common priesthood together. But above all Christian marriage and the family draw their strength from the Eucharist. The Council described this sacrament as "the source and summit" of the Church's life†—that is, everything in the Church flows from the Eucharist and everything is ordered to participation in it. Echoing this teaching, Saint John Paul II says here that "the Eucharist is the very source of Christian marriage" (*FC* no. 57).

The kingship of the Christian family, like that of its Lord, is exercised as service. An ancient Christian axiom proclaims,

---

* See, for example, his weekly general audience of July 4, 1984.

† See *Lumen Gentium*, no. 11.

"To serve is to reign." This is lived out in the myriad of everyday activities of care and love within the household. Work, preparing food, caring for the sick, juggling schedules, carpooling—this is the stuff of the family's kingly office. These humble day-to-day activities, symbolized in the very ordinary gifts of bread and wine, are offered to God in the Church's Eucharistic worship and are thus transformed into Christ's living presence among us.

1. What does being called to holiness in your state in life mean to you? Do you see family as an obstacle or an opportunity to respond to this call?

2. Pope Francis has urged the Church to become a missionary Church and a "Church which goes forth" (see *Evangelii Gaudium*, nos. 19–20, 27). What does this mean for the Christian family, which is a domestic church? How can families become subjects and not merely objects of evangelization?

3. Saint John Paul II describes the importance of parents being models and educators in prayer for their children (*FC* nos. 59–60). How would you describe the place that prayer had in your family when you were a child? What role does personal, communal, and liturgical prayer play in your life as a Christian today?

4. How is the Eucharist the source and summit of your family's life of prayer?

Saint John Paul II gave a great gift to the Church when he introduced the luminous mysteries of the rosary in his Apostolic Letter *Rosarium Virginis Mariae* (2002). These mysteries not only give us the opportunity to ponder our Lord's life and ministry, but each in their own way can shed light on the family's vocation as a domestic church. Pray these mysteries and allow the Holy Spirit to deepen your understanding of the call to holiness given to the Christian family:

The Baptism in the Jordan—Our baptism into Christ is the foundation of our call to holiness. It is also the basis of the priesthood of Christians, which enable men and women to confer the sacrament of Marriage on one another.

The Wedding Feast of Cana—The presence of Christ the Bridegroom transforms the water of the Old Law, which could not cleanse, into the new and more excellent wine of marriage lived in the Holy Spirit.

The Preaching of the Kingdom—In its prophetic office the Christian family is called to announce the good news of our salvation in Christ.

The Transfiguration—Families allow the glory of Christ's holiness to shine through them in learning to seek reconciliation and live in mutual love every day.

The Gift of the Eucharist—Christ's ongoing presence in the sacrifice of the Mass is the source and summit of the whole of the Christian family's life.

Act

Make an honest assessment of your own prayer life and that of your family (if you are living in a family). What are you doing well? What could you be doing better? Discuss your assessment with the other members of your household and get their input. What changes can you make to better live out your priestly office together?

PART FOUR

Pastoral Care of the Family: Stages, Structures, Agents, and Situations

I. STAGES OF PASTORAL CARE OF THE FAMILY

The Church accompanies the Christian family on its journey through life

65. Like every other living reality, the family too is called upon to develop and grow. After the preparation of engagement and the sacramental celebration of marriage, the couple begin their daily journey toward the progressive actuation of the values and duties of marriage itself.

In the light of faith and by virtue of hope, the Christian family too shares, in communion with the Church, in the experience of the earthly pilgrimage toward the full revelation and manifestation of the Kingdom of God.

Therefore, it must be emphasized once more that the pastoral intervention of the Church in support of the family is a matter of urgency. Every effort should be made to strengthen and develop pastoral care for the family, which should be treated as a real matter of priority, in the certainty that future evangelization depends largely on the domestic church.[165]

The Church's pastoral concern will not be limited only to the Christian families closest at hand; it will extend its horizons in harmony with the Heart of Christ, and will show itself to be even more lively for families in general and for those families in particular which are in difficult or irregular situations. For all of them the Church will have a word of truth, goodness, understanding, hope, and deep sympathy with their sometimes tragic difficulties. To all of them she will offer her disinterested help so that they can come closer to that model of a family which the Creator intended from "the beginning" and which Christ has renewed with his redeeming grace.

The Church's pastoral action must be progressive, also in the sense that it must follow the family, accompanying it step by step in the different stages of its formation and development.

Preparation for marriage

66. More than ever necessary in our times is preparation of young people for marriage and family life. In some countries it is still the families themselves that, according to ancient customs, ensure the passing on to young people of the values concerning married and family life, and they do this through

a gradual process of education or initiation. But the changes that have taken place within almost all modern societies demand that not only the family but also society and the Church should be involved in the effort of properly preparing young people for their future responsibilities. Many negative phenomena which are today noted with regret in family life derive from the fact that, in the new situations, young people not only lose sight of the correct hierarchy of values but, since they no longer have certain criteria of behavior, they do not know how to face and deal with the new difficulties. But experience teaches that young people who have been well prepared for family life generally succeed better than others.

This is even more applicable to Christian marriage, which influences the holiness of large numbers of men and women. The Church must therefore promote better and more intensive programs of marriage preparation, in order to eliminate as far as possible the difficulties that many married couples find themselves in, and even more in order to favor positively the establishing and maturing of successful marriages.

Marriage preparation has to be seen and put into practice as a gradual and continuous process. It includes three main stages: remote, proximate, and immediate preparation.

Remote preparation begins in early childhood, in that wise family training which leads children to discover themselves as being endowed with a rich and complex psychology and with a particular personality with its own strengths and weaknesses. It is the period when esteem for all authentic human values is instilled, both in interpersonal and in social relationships, with all that this signifies for the formation of character, for the control and right use of one's inclinations, for the manner of regarding and meeting people of the opposite sex, and so on. Also necessary, especially for Christians, is solid spiritual and catechetical formation that will show that marriage is a true vocation and mission, without excluding the possibility of the total gift of self to God in the vocation to the priestly or religious life.

Upon this basis there will subsequently and gradually be built up the *proximate preparation*, which—from the suitable age and with adequate catechesis, as in a catechumenal process—involves a more specific preparation for the sacraments, as it were, a rediscovery of them. This renewed catechesis of young people and others preparing for Christian marriage is absolutely necessary in order that the sacrament may be celebrated and lived with the right moral and spiritual dispositions. The religious formation of young people should be integrated, at the right moment and in accordance with the various concrete requirements, with a preparation for life as a couple. This preparation will present marriage as an interpersonal relationship of a man and a woman that has to be continually developed, and it will encourage those concerned to study the nature of conjugal sexuality and responsible parenthood, with the essential medical and biological knowledge connected with it. It will also acquaint those concerned with correct methods for the education of children, and will assist them in gaining the basic requisites for well-ordered family life, such as stable work, sufficient financial resources, sensible administration, notions of housekeeping.

Finally, one must not overlook preparation for the family apostolate, for fraternal solidarity and collaboration with other families, for active membership in groups, associations, movements, and undertakings set up for the human and Christian benefit of the family.

The *immediate preparation* for the celebration of the sacrament of Matrimony should take place in the months and weeks immediately preceding the wedding, so as to give a new meaning, content, and form to the so-called premarital enquiry required by Canon Law. This preparation is not only necessary in every case, but is also more urgently needed for engaged couples that still manifest shortcomings or difficulties in Christian doctrine and practice.

Among the elements to be instilled in this journey of faith, which is similar to the catechumenate, there must also be a deeper knowledge of the mystery of Christ and the Church, of the meaning of grace and of the responsibility of Christian marriage, as well as preparation for taking an active and conscious part in the rites of the marriage liturgy.

The Christian family and the whole of the ecclesial community should feel involved in the different phases of the preparation for marriage, which have been described only in their broad outlines. It is to be hoped that the episcopal conferences, just as they are concerned with appropriate initiatives to help engaged couples to be more aware of the seriousness of their choice and also to help pastors of souls to make sure of the couples' proper dispositions, so they will also take steps to see that there is issued a *Directory for the Pastoral Care of the*

Family. In this they should lay down, in the first place, the minimum content, duration, and method of the "Preparation Courses," balancing the different aspects—doctrinal, pedagogical, legal, and medical—concerning marriage, and structuring them in such a way that those preparing for marriage will not only receive an intellectual training but will also feel a desire to enter actively into the ecclesial community.

Although one must not underestimate the necessity and obligation of the immediate preparation for marriage—which would happen if dispensations from it were easily given—nevertheless such preparation must always be set forth and put into practice in such a way that omitting it is not an impediment to the celebration of marriage.

The celebration

67. Christian marriage normally requires a liturgical celebration expressing in social and community form the essentially ecclesial and sacramental nature of the conjugal covenant between baptized persons.

Inasmuch as it is a *sacramental action of sanctification*, the celebration of marriage—inserted into the liturgy, which is the summit of the Church's action and the source of her sanctifying power[166]—must be *per se* valid, worthy, and fruitful. This opens a wide field for pastoral solicitude, in order that the needs deriving from the nature of the conjugal covenant, elevated into a sacrament, may be fully met, and also in order that the Church's discipline regarding free consent, impediments, the canonical form, and the actual rite of the celebration may be faithfully observed. The celebration should be simple and dignified, according to the norms of the competent authorities of the Church. It is also for them—in accordance with concrete circumstances of time and place and in conformity with the norms issued by the Apostolic See[167]—to include in the liturgical celebration such elements proper to each culture which serve to express more clearly the profound human and religious significance of the marriage contract, provided that such elements contain nothing that is not in harmony with Christian faith and morality.

Inasmuch as it is a *sign*, the liturgical celebration should be conducted in such a way as to constitute, also in its external reality, a proclamation of the word of God and a profession of faith on the part of the community of believers. Pastoral commitment will be expressed here through the intelligent and careful preparation of the Liturgy of the Word and through the education to faith of those participating in the celebration and in the first place the couple being married.

Inasmuch as it is a *sacramental action of the Church*, the liturgical celebration of marriage should involve the Christian community, with the full, active, and responsible participation of all those present, according to the place and task of each individual: the bride and bridegroom, the priest, the witnesses, the relatives, the friends, the other members of the faithful, all of them members of an assembly that manifests and lives the mystery of Christ and his Church. For the celebration of Christian marriage in the sphere of ancestral cultures or traditions, the principles laid down above should be followed.

Celebration of marriage and evangelization of non-believing baptized persons

68. Precisely because in the celebration of the sacrament very special attention must be devoted to the moral and spiritual dispositions of those being married, in particular to their faith, we must here deal with a not infrequent difficulty in which the pastors of the Church can find themselves in the context of our secularized society.

In fact, the faith of the person asking the Church for marriage can exist in different degrees, and it is the primary duty of pastors to bring about a rediscovery of this faith and to nourish it and bring it to maturity. But pastors must also understand the reasons that lead the Church also to admit to the celebration of marriage those who are imperfectly disposed.

The sacrament of Matrimony has this specific element that distinguishes it from all the other sacraments: it is the sacrament of something that was part of the very economy of creation; it is the very conjugal covenant instituted by the Creator "in the beginning." Therefore the decision of a man and a woman to marry in accordance with this divine plan, that is to say, the decision to commit by their irrevocable conjugal consent their whole lives in indissoluble love and unconditional fidelity, really involves, even if not in a fully conscious way, an attitude of profound obedience to the will of God, an attitude which cannot exist without God's grace. They have thus already begun what is in a true and proper sense a journey toward salvation, a journey which the celebration of the sacrament and the immediate preparation for it can complement and bring to completion, given the uprightness of their intention.

On the other hand it is true that in some places engaged couples ask to be married in church for motives which are social rather than genuinely religious. This is not surprising. Marriage, in fact, is not an event that concerns only the persons actually getting married. By its very nature it is also a social matter, committing the couple being married in the eyes of society. And its celebration has always been an occasion of rejoicing that brings together families and friends. It therefore goes without saying that social as well as personal motives enter into the request to be married in church.

Nevertheless, it must not be forgotten that these engaged couples, by virtue of their Baptism, are already really sharers in Christ's marriage covenant with the Church, and that, by their right intention, they have accepted God's plan regarding marriage and therefore at least implicitly consent to what the Church intends to do when she celebrates marriage. Thus, the fact that motives of a social nature also enter into the request is not enough to justify refusal on the part of pastors. Moreover, as the Second Vatican Council teaches, the sacraments by words and ritual elements nourish and strengthen faith:[168] that faith toward which the married couple are already journeying by reason of the uprightness of their intention, which Christ's grace certainly does not fail to favor and support.

As for wishing to lay down further criteria for admission to the ecclesial celebration of marriage, criteria that would concern the level of faith of those to be married, this would above all involve grave risks. In the first place, the risk of making unfounded and discriminatory judgments; secondly, the risk of causing doubts about the validity of marriages already celebrated, with grave harm to Christian communities, and new and unjustified anxieties to the consciences of married couples; one would also fall into the danger of calling into question the sacramental nature of many marriages of brethren separated from full communion with the Catholic Church, thus contradicting ecclesial tradition.

However, when in spite of all efforts, engaged couples show that they reject explicitly and formally what the Church intends to do when the marriage of baptized persons is celebrated, the pastor of souls cannot admit them to the celebration of marriage. In spite of his reluctance to do so, he has the duty to take note of the situation and to make it clear to those concerned that, in these circumstances, it is not the Church that is placing an obstacle in the way of the celebration that they are asking for, but themselves.

Once more there appears in all its urgency the need for evangelization and catechesis before and after marriage, effected by the whole Christian community, so that every man and woman that gets married celebrates the sacrament of Matrimony not only validly but also fruitfully.

Pastoral care after marriage

69. The pastoral care of the regularly established family signifies, in practice, the commitment of all the members of the local ecclesial community to helping the couple to discover and live their new vocation and mission. In order that

the family may be ever more a true community of love, it is necessary that all its members should be helped and trained in their responsibilities as they face the new problems that arise, in mutual service, and in active sharing in family life.

This holds true especially for young families, which, finding themselves in a context of new values and responsibilities, are more vulnerable, especially in the first years of marriage, to possible difficulties, such as those created by adaptation to life together or by the birth of children. Young married couples should learn to accept willingly, and make good use of, the discreet, tactful, and generous help offered by other couples that already have more experience of married and family life. Thus, within the ecclesial community—the great family made up of Christian families—there will take place a mutual exchange of presence and help among all the families, each one putting at the service of others its own experience of life, as well as the gifts of faith and grace. Animated by a true apostolic spirit, this assistance from family to family will constitute one of the simplest, most effective, and most accessible means for transmitting from one to another those Christian values which are both the starting point and goal of all pastoral care. Thus young families will not limit themselves merely to receiving, but in their turn, having been helped in this way, will become a source of enrichment for other longer established families, through their witness of life and practical contribution.

In her pastoral care of young families, the Church must also pay special attention to helping them to live married love responsibly in relationship with its demands of communion and service to life. She must likewise help them to harmonize the intimacy of home life with the generous shared work of building up the Church and society. When children are born and the married couple becomes a family in the full and specific sense, the Church will still remain close to the parents in order that they may accept their children and love them as a gift received from the Lord of life, and joyfully accept the task of serving them in their human and Christian growth.

Ponder

Having the opportunity to work with seminarians who are preparing for a lifelong vocation to the priesthood enables us to see the alarming contrast between seminary training and marriage preparation programs. On the one hand, seminarians may spend six to ten years preparing for their ordination, doing intensive study, pastoral training, and personal formation. On the other hand, engaged couples who are also preparing for a demanding, lifelong vocation might complete their preparation in as little as six months. Often most of this time is devoted to planning a wedding, which will be over and done in a day. The actual preparation for marriage might be condensed into a weekend or a few evening meetings.

Saint John Paul II clearly saw the need to rethink marriage preparation and to intensify the Church's efforts in this area. Preparation for a lasting vocation, which is integral to the life of the Church and to society, requires formation that takes place over years, not weeks. He therefore challenged us to think of marriage preparation as beginning early in a child's life and lasting until the wedding. He identified the stages in this process as remote, proximate, and immediate preparation.

Remote preparation for a vocation begins early, when little children learn basic human values. In being raised in a Christian family, they come to understand their own dignity, including the way that it is reflected in their bodies. They learn how to receive and to give love and to treat others justly. They also learn respect for the dignity of other persons, both of their own sex and the opposite sex, and the reality of God and God's call in their lives. All of these lay a foundation for their future ability to discern and pursue their vocation.

Proximate preparation builds on this foundation with more explicit catechesis. Since most children are baptized as infants, they are catechized as they prepare for the sacraments of Reconciliation, Eucharist, and Confirmation. As they mature into adolescence, this catechesis should treat more clearly the gift of sexuality, the meaning and nature of marriage, and the way in which marriage and virginity or religious celibacy are complementary vocations. As Saint John Paul II would later teach, "There can be no avoiding the duty to offer, especially to adolescents and young adults, an authentic education in sexuality and in love, an education which involves training in chastity as a virtue which fosters personal maturity and makes one capable of respecting the 'spousal' meaning of the body."[*]

Immediate preparation is given in the months and weeks before the wedding—what we normally think of as marriage preparation. However, it is clear to us, from our over twenty years of preparing couples for marriage, that if this is the only preparation couple's receive, it will not be adequate. This

---

[*] *Evangelium Vitae*, no. 97. The citation is from http://www.vatican.va/holy_father/john_paul_ii/encyclicals/documents/hf_jp-ii_enc_25031995_evangelium-vitae_en.html (accessed 9/20/14). The Pontifical Council for the Family provided an outstanding description of what such age-appropriate formation looks like in its 1995 document *The Truth and Meaning of Human Sexuality*.

preparation is itself a form of evangelization, especially for unbaptized persons or nominal Christians who approach the Church for marriage. The Church is also realizing that vocational formation for marriage cannot stop at the wedding. John Paul II also speaks to this need for pastoral care after marriage (see *FC* no. 69). We need "post-Cana" programs to provide ongoing formation and support to couples to help them succeed in an increasingly anti-marriage culture.

1. Did the catechesis you received as a child lay a foundation for you to understand and discern God's call in your life? How?

2. The Rite of Baptism says that parents are "the first teachers of their child in the ways of the faith."* What are some of the ways parents can fulfill this role as they raise their children?

3. Why is it important for those engaged in preparing couples for marriage to realize that this is an opportunity for evangelization?

4. Does your parish and diocese offer opportunities for ongoing support and formation for married couples? What forms does this take? What additional activities and events could be added to strengthen existing marriages?

---

* The phrase is from the blessing of the child's father at the end of the (1970) rite. The text is available at: http://www.catholicliturgy.com/index.cfm/fuseaction/textcontents/index/4/subindex/67/textindex/7 (accessed 11/7/14).

PRAY

Prayerfully read the prayer of Tobias (Tb 8:5–8):

"Blessed are you, O God of our ancestors;
blessed be your name forever and ever!
Let the heavens and all your creation bless you forever.
You made Adam, and you made his wife Eve
to be his helper and support;
and from these two the human race has come.
You said, 'It is not good for the man to be alone;
let us make him a helper like himself.'
Now, not with lust,
but with fidelity I take this kinswoman as my wife.
Send down your mercy on me and on her,
and grant that we may grow old together.
Bless us with children.
They said together, "Amen, amen!"

What does this prayer teach you about marriage and its purposes? About good marriage preparation? Spend time praying for those who are preparing for marriage (at any stage of life), and for the lay men and women, religious, deacons, priests, and bishops who prepare them, that they might effectively communicate the beauty of God's design for marriage.

ACT

The U.S. bishops have a wonderful Web site full of resources for those preparing for marriage and those already married (see http://www.foryourmarriage.org/). Spend some time looking over the Web site. Make sure to note things that could be helpful for your own marriage or ministry.

II. Structures of Family Pastoral Care

Pastoral activity is always the dynamic expression of the reality of the Church, committed to her mission of salvation. Family pastoral care too—which is a particular and specific form of pastoral activity—has as its operative principle and responsible agent the Church herself, through her structures and workers.

The ecclesial community and in particular the parish

70. The Church, which is at the same time a saved and a saving community, has to be considered here under two aspects: as universal and particular. The second aspect is expressed and actuated in the diocesan community, which is pastorally divided into lesser communities, of which the parish is of special importance.

Communion with the universal Church does not hinder but rather guarantees and promotes the substance and originality of the various particular Churches. These latter remain the more immediate and more effective subjects of operation for putting the pastoral care of the family into practice. In this sense every local Church and, in more particular terms, every parochial community must become more vividly aware of the grace and responsibility that it receives from the Lord in order that it may promote the pastoral care of the family. No plan for organized pastoral work, at any level, must ever fail to take into consideration the pastoral care of the family.

Also to be seen in the light of this responsibility is the importance of the proper preparation of all those who will be more specifically engaged in this kind of apostolate. Priests and men and women religious, from the time of their formation, should be oriented and trained progressively and thoroughly for the various tasks. Among the various initiatives I am pleased to emphasize the recent establishment in Rome, at the Pontifical Lateran University, of a higher institute for the study of the problems of the family. Institutes of this kind have also been set up in some dioceses. Bishops should see to it that as many priests as possible attend specialized courses there before taking on parish responsibilities. Elsewhere, formation courses are periodically held at higher institutes of theological and pastoral studies. Such initiatives should be encouraged, sustained, increased in number, and of course are also open to lay people who intend to use their professional skills (medical, legal, psychological, social, or educational) to help the family.

The family

71. But it is especially necessary to recognize the unique place that, in this field, belongs to the mission of married couples and Christian families, by virtue of the grace received in the sacrament. This mission must be placed at the service of the building up of the Church, the establishing of the Kingdom of God in history. This is demanded as an act of docile obedience to Christ the Lord. For it is he who, by virtue of the fact that marriage of baptized persons has been raised to a sacrament,

confers upon Christian married couples a special mission as apostles, sending them as workers into his vineyard, and, in a very special way, into this field of the family.

In this activity, married couples act in communion and collaboration with the other members of the Church, who also work for the family, contributing their own gifts and ministries. This apostolate will be exercised in the first place within the families of those concerned, through the witness of a life lived in conformity with the divine law in all its aspects, through the Christian formation of the children, through helping them to mature in faith, through education to chastity, through preparation for life, through vigilance in protecting them from the ideological and moral dangers with which they are often threatened, through their gradual and responsible inclusion in the ecclesial community and the civil community, through help and advice in choosing a vocation, through mutual help among family members for human and Christian growth together, and so on. The apostolate of the family will also become wider through works of spiritual and material charity toward other families, especially those most in need of help and support, toward the poor, the sick, the old, the handicapped, orphans, widows, spouses that have been abandoned, unmarried mothers and mothers-to-be in difficult situations who are tempted to have recourse to abortion, and so on.

Associations of families for families

72. Still within the Church, which is the subject responsible for the pastoral care of the family, mention should be

made of the various groupings of members of the faithful in which the mystery of Christ's Church is in some measure manifested and lived. One should therefore recognize and make good use of—each one in relationship to its own characteristics, purposes, effectiveness, and methods—the different ecclesial communities, the various groups and the numerous movements engaged in various ways, for different reasons and at different levels, in the pastoral care of the family.

For this reason the Synod expressly recognized the useful contribution made by such associations of spirituality, formation, and apostolate. It will be their task to foster among the faithful a lively sense of solidarity, to favor a manner of living inspired by the Gospel and by the faith of the Church, to form consciences according to Christian values and not according to the standards of public opinion, to stimulate people to perform works of charity for one another and for others with a spirit of openness which will make Christian families into a true source of light and a wholesome leaven for other families.

It is similarly desirable that, with a lively sense of the common good, Christian families should become actively engaged, at every level, in other non-ecclesial associations as well. Some of these associations work for the preservation, transmission, and protection of the wholesome ethical and cultural values of each people, the development of the human person, the medical, juridical, and social protection of mothers and young children, the just advancement of women and the struggle against all that is detrimental to their dignity, the increase of mutual solidarity, knowledge of the problems connected with the responsible regulation of fertility in accordance with natural methods that are in conformity with human dignity and the teaching of the Church. Other associations work for the building of a more just and human world; for the promotion of just laws favoring the right social order with full respect for the dignity and every legitimate freedom of the individual and the family, on both the national and international level; for collaboration with the school and with the other institutions that complete the education of children, and so forth.

Ponder

From the beginning of its history, the Church has recognized the importance of involving the local Church in the marriage of its members. Like most of their contemporaries, the earliest Christians typically celebrated weddings as family events in their homes. Nevertheless, at the beginning of the second century, on his way to his martyrdom in Rome, Saint Ignatius of Antioch told his fellow bishop Polycarp that Christians should not marry each other without the consent of their local bishop.[*] In the fourth and fifth centuries the Eastern churches developed the rite of crowning for couples when they attended the liturgy for the first time after their wedding. By the seventh century the celebration of weddings in the East took place in a church before a priest or bishop. The Western church followed a similar path some centuries later.

Why did the Church see the need for this growing involvement in the marriages and family lives of its members? As Saint John Paul II explains, it is because the Church sees the pastoral care of the family as part of "her mission of salvation" (*FC*, introduction to section II of Part IV). This pastoral care involves the Church at all levels. The universal Church shapes this effort through its teaching ministry and by setting

---

[*] See his *Letter to Polycarp* (c. 117 A.D.), 5.2.

pastoral priorities for the Church as a whole. The local churches, under the leadership of the bishop, apply this teaching and pastoral care to the needs of their own people and ensure communion with the wider Church. The primary place where most Catholics encounter this pastoral care is in their parishes under the direction of their pastors. John Paul II underscores the importance of specialized study and ongoing formation for priests and men and women religious who interact with married couples and their families.

Yet the Holy Father recognized that priests and religious in parish settings cannot do it all. The primary and most effective agents of the Church in the pastoral care of families are lay people and families themselves. As John Paul II teaches, the sacrament of Marriage "confers upon Christian married couples a special mission as apostles, sending them as workers into his vineyard, and, in a very special way, into this field of the family" (*FC* no. 71). This is true first of all for parents in their own families, and it is also true of their ministry to others. Mentor couples can provide an invaluable service in working with and supporting engaged and newly married couples. In collaboration with the work of priests and religious, lay ministry for marriage and family can increase the reach and effectiveness of pastoral care. And beyond the parish, associations of families and lay ecclesial movements can provide a richer witness of family life and further opportunities to build Christian community.

1. Why is it important to understand that your local parish and diocese is a part of the universal Church? Where do you see this reality acknowledged in the

liturgy? Where else do you experience this communion with the wider Church?

2. What forms of marriage and family ministry have you experienced in the Church? Which of these have been most fruitful for you and why?

3. What does it mean to you that your baptism gives you a share in the priesthood of Christ and enables you to actively serve the Church? To what ministries do you give your time, talent, and treasure in order to live out this office?

Pray

Saint Paul uses the analogy of a body with many parts to communicate his understanding of the importance and interdependence of each member of the Church. Prayerfully read his teaching on this topic in 1 Corinthians 12:12–30. Ask our Lord to show you how you might better use your gifts to build up the life of your parish and diocese.

Act

Find out what marriage and family-related ministries your parish has. Spend time praying about how you might support one of these ministries through your talent, treasure, or time— even if it is just making a commitment to pray for the ministry on a regular basis. If there are none, discern in prayer if the Lord may be leading you to start one, and if so, discuss it with your pastor.

III. Agents of the Pastoral Care of the Family

As well as the family, which is the object but above all the subject of pastoral care of the family, one must also mention the other main agents in this particular sector.

Bishops and priests

73. The person principally responsible in the diocese for the pastoral care of the family is the bishop. As father and pastor, he must exercise particular solicitude in this clearly priority sector of pastoral care. He must devote to it personal interest, care, time, personnel, and resources, but above all personal support for the families and for all those who, in the various diocesan structures, assist him in the pastoral care of the family. It will be his particular care to make the diocese ever more truly a "diocesan family," a model and source of hope for the many families that belong to it. The setting up of the Pontifical Council for the Family is to be seen in this light: to be a sign of the importance that I attribute to pastoral care for the family in the world, and at the same time to be an effective instrument for aiding and promoting it at every level.

The bishops avail themselves especially of the priests, whose task—as the Synod expressly emphasized—constitutes an essential part of the Church's ministry regarding marriage and the family. The same is true of deacons to whose care this sector of pastoral work may be entrusted.

Their responsibility extends not only to moral and liturgical matters but to personal and social matters as well. They must support the family in its difficulties and sufferings, caring for its members and helping them to see their lives in the light of the Gospel. It is not superfluous to note that from this mission, if it is exercised with due discernment and with a truly apostolic spirit, the minister of the Church draws fresh encouragement and spiritual energy for his own vocation too, and for the exercise of his ministry.

Priests and deacons, when they have received timely and serious preparation for this apostolate, must unceasingly act toward families as fathers, brothers, pastors, and teachers, assisting them with the means of grace and enlightening them with the light of truth. Their teaching and advice must therefore always be in full harmony with the authentic Magisterium of the Church, in such a way as to help the People of God to gain a correct sense of the faith, to be subsequently applied to practical life. Such fidelity to the Magisterium will also enable priests to make every effort to be united in their judgments, in order to avoid troubling the consciences of the faithful.

In the Church, the pastors and the laity share in the prophetic mission of Christ: the laity do so by witnessing to the faith by their words and by their Christian lives; the pastors do so by distinguishing in that witness what is the expression of genuine faith from what is less in harmony with the light of faith; the family, as a Christian community, does so through its special sharing and witness of faith. Thus there begins a dialogue also between pastors and families. Theologians and experts in family matters can be of great help in this dialogue, by explaining exactly the content of the Church's Magisterium and the content of the experience of family life. In this way the teaching of the Magisterium becomes better understood and the way is opened to its progressive development. But it is useful to recall that the proximate and obligatory norm in the teaching of the faith—also concerning family matters—belongs to the hierarchical Magisterium. Clearly defined relationships between theologians, experts in family matters, and the Magisterium are of no little assistance for the correct understanding of the faith and for promoting—within the boundaries of the faith—legitimate pluralism.

Men and women religious

74. The contribution that can be made to the apostolate of the family by men and women religious and consecrated persons in general finds its primary, fundamental, and original expression precisely in their consecration to God. By reason of this consecration, "for all Christ's faithful religious recall that wonderful marriage made by God, which will be fully manifested in the future age, and in which the Church has Christ for her only spouse,"[169] and they are witnesses to that universal charity which, through chastity embraced for the Kingdom of heaven, makes them ever more available to dedicate themselves generously to the service of God and to the works of the apostolate.

Hence the possibility for men and women religious, and members of secular institutes and other institutes of perfection, either individually or in groups, to develop their service to families, with particular solicitude for children, especially if they are abandoned, unwanted, orphaned, poor, or handicapped. They can also visit families and look after the sick; they can foster relationships of respect and charity toward one-parent families or families that are in difficulties or are separated; they can offer their own work of teaching and counseling in the preparation of young people for marriage, and in helping couples toward truly responsible parenthood; they can open their own houses for simple and cordial hospitality, so that families can find there the sense of God's presence and gain a taste for prayer and recollection, and see the practical examples of lives lived in charity and fraternal joy as members of the larger family of God.

I would like to add a most pressing exhortation to the heads of institutes of consecrated life to consider—always with substantial respect for the proper and original charism of each one—the apostolate of the family as one of the priority tasks, rendered even more urgent by the present state of the world.

Lay specialists

75. Considerable help can be given to families by lay specialists (doctors, lawyers, psychologists, social workers, consultants, etc.) who either as individuals or as members of various associations and undertakings offer their contribution of enlightenment, advice, orientation, and support. To these people one can well apply the exhortations that I had the occasion to address to the Confederation of Family Advisory

Bureaus of Christian Inspiration: "Yours is a commitment that well deserves the title of mission, so noble are the aims that it pursues, and so determining, for the good of society and the Christian community itself, are the results that derive from it. . . . All that you succeed in doing to support the family is destined to have an effectiveness that goes beyond its own sphere and reaches other people too and has an effect on society The future of the world and of the Church passes through the family."[170]

Recipients and agents of social communications

76. This very important category in modern life deserves a word of its own. It is well known that the means of social communication "affect, and often profoundly, the minds of those who use them, under the affective and intellectual aspect and also under the moral and religious aspect," especially in the case of young people.[171] They can thus exercise a beneficial influence on the life and habits of the family and on the education of children, but at the same time they also conceal "snares and dangers that cannot be ignored."[172] They could also become a vehicle—sometimes cleverly and systematically manipulated, as unfortunately happens in various countries of the world—for divisive ideologies and distorted ways of looking at life, the family, religion, and morality, attitudes that lack respect for man's true dignity and destiny.

This danger is all the more real inasmuch as "the modern life style—especially in the more industrialized nations—all too often causes families to abandon their responsibility to educate their children. Evasion of this duty is made easy for them by the presence of television and certain publications in the home, and in this way they keep their children's time and energies occupied."[173] Hence "the duty . . . to protect the young from the forms of aggression they are subjected to by the mass media," and to ensure that the use of the media in the family is carefully regulated. Families should also take care to seek for their children other forms of entertainment that are more wholesome, useful, and physically, morally, and spiritually formative, "to develop and use to advantage the free time of the young and direct their energies."[174]

Furthermore, because the means of social communication, like the school and the environment, often have a notable influence on the formation of children, parents as recipients must actively ensure the moderate, critical, watchful, and prudent use of the media, by discovering what effect they have on their children and by controlling the use of the media in such a way as to "train the conscience of their children to express calm and objective judgments, which will then guide them in the choice or rejection of programs available."[175]

With equal commitment parents will endeavor to influence the selection and the preparation of the programs themselves, by keeping in contact—through suitable initiatives—with those in charge of the various phases of production and transmission. In this way they will ensure that the fundamental human values that form part of the true good of society are not ignored or deliberately attacked. Rather they will ensure the broadcasting of programs that present in the right light family problems and their proper solution. In this regard my venerated predecessor Paul VI wrote: "Producers must know and respect the needs of the family, and this sometimes presupposes in them true courage, and always a high sense of responsibility. In fact they are expected to avoid anything that could harm the family in its existence, its stability, its balance, and its happiness. Every attack on the fundamental value of the family—meaning eroticism or violence, the defense of divorce or of antisocial attitudes among young people—is an attack on the true good of man."[176]

I myself, on a similar occasion, pointed out that families "to a considerable extent need to be able to count on the good will, integrity, and sense of responsibility of the media professionals—publishers, writers, producers, directors, playwrights, newsmen, commentators, and actors."[177] It is therefore also the duty of the Church to continue to devote every care to these categories, at the same time encouraging and supporting Catholics who feel the call and have the necessary talents, to take up this sensitive type of work.

Having looked at the structures through which the Church ministers to the family, Saint John Paul II turns his attention to the persons who direct these structures. Bishops have primary responsibility for the pastoral care of their dioceses. They should aim to exercise their ministry so as to build a "diocesan family" that can inspire the Christian families who belong to it (*FC* no. 73). Priests and deacons, under the guidance of the local bishop, exercise a "fatherly role" within their parish communities. The Church's ordained ministers are assisted in their pastoral care of families by the valuable work of others—theologians, men and women religious, and lay specialists whose expertise can help pastors better understand families and the challenges they face.

Tucked within a single section (no. 76) is a reflection on the impact of social communications (i.e., the media) on the family. Karol Wojtyła understood the importance of this topic due to his background as a playwright, the propaganda he faced from the hostile communist government in Poland, the Second Vatican Council's decree on the media,[*] and his own observation of the twentieth century. In this section John Paul II acknowledges the potential impact of the media on the

---

[*] See the *Decree on the Media of Social Communications* (*Inter Mirifica*) (1963).

personalities of people—especially the young. This impact is not only on their minds and emotions, but also on their moral and religious outlook. While the influence can be beneficial, the Holy Father warns that it can also contain "snares and dangers that cannot be ignored." This requires that parents be vigilant.

His warning echoes even more loudly in our own day. If our twenty-first-century culture has been shaped for good and for ill by the Industrial Revolution, and wounded by the sexual revolution, it is being transformed before our eyes by the exponential growth of technology—especially information and communication technology. Now it is not only movies, music, and television that reach into the home and form the culture of our families. Today the internet, cell phones, and social media shape the lives of young people—often faster than their parents can react.

To take just one example of the havoc being wrought today by the dark side of technology, consider the case of pornography. Saint John Paul II identified it as an offense against women's dignity (no. 24). Certainly in the 1980s pornography was beginning to change from a furtive underground business to a very lucrative public industry in slick magazines and videos. However, the internet exponentially expanded the reach of this poison into people's homes and hearts, creating havoc in families. Children with Internet access are exposed to sexually explicit material at much younger ages. Pornography objectifies persons, and this is reinforced by the popular culture in music, visual media, and perverse practices such as "sexting." By some estimates, sexual addiction to some form of pornography is involved in over half the divorces in the United States.[*]

The answer to these threats is not to shrink back from the culture or new technology. Instead, the answer is to realize that this technology and our wounded culture need the healing power of the Gospel to realize their potential for good. The tasks of the family as a domestic church can only be accomplished in the power of the Holy Spirit.

1. The Old Testament presents God as a loving, protecting, and nurturing Father to the people of Israel. In light of this portrayal, how do you understand John Paul II's encouragement to bishops, priests, and deacons, to exercise a "fatherly role" in their pastoral ministry?

2. How has modern communication technology and the media improved your life and that of your family? In what ways have they undermined your time for each other and your ability to communicate in depth? How can you improve your use of the media so that it benefits your family in a healthy way?"

3. Pope John Paul II encourages Catholics to pursue careers as media professionals and artists to help shape the culture in positive ways (see no. 76). Can you think of examples of books, plays, movies, or music produced

---

[*] See Catherine Briggs, "Porn Use Can Lead to Divorce: Study" (July 9, 2014). Available at: https://www.lifesitenews.com/news/porn-use-can-lead-to-divorce-study (accessed 11/7/14).

by Christians that have had a positive impact on you and your family?

4. In his catecheses on the body, Saint John Paul II reflected at length on the beatitude "blessed are the clean of heart" (Mt 5:8). What steps can you take as a person, a spouse, or a parent to live this beatitude? How can you guard yourself and your family in a culture that often bombards those in it with media images that offend the dignity of persons and the beauty of the vocation of marriage?

Pray

Pray the sorrowful mysteries of the rosary, pondering our Lord's suffering for our sins. Reflect on the depth of the merciful love he displayed for us in his passion. Offer the rosary in reparation for the violations of human dignity, human life, marriage, and family within our culture, and for the healing of those wounded by these offenses.

Act

The Church still commends Fridays to her members as a day of penance in which we recall the Lord's passion. Offer whatever form of penance you observe on Friday for the transformation of our culture—that it might be "evangelized in depth" (*FC* no. 8). Ask Saint John Paul II to pray with you for this intention.

IV. Pastoral Care of the Family in Difficult Cases

Particular circumstances

77. An even more generous, intelligent, and prudent pastoral commitment, modeled on the Good Shepherd, is called for in the case of families which, often independently of their own wishes and through pressures of various other kinds, find themselves faced by situations which are objectively difficult.

In this regard it is necessary to call special attention to certain particular groups which are more in need not only of assistance but also of more incisive action upon public opinion and especially upon cultural, economic, and juridical structures, in order that the profound causes of their needs may be eliminated as far as possible.

Such for example are the families of migrant workers; the families of those obliged to be away for long periods, such as members of the armed forces, sailors, and all kinds of itinerant people; the families of those in prison, of refugees, and exiles; the families in big cities living practically speaking as outcasts; families with no home; incomplete or single parent families; families with children that are handicapped or addicted to drugs; the families of alcoholics; families that have been uprooted from their cultural and social environment or are in danger of losing it; families discriminated against for political or other reasons; families that are ideologically divided; families that are unable to make ready contact with the parish; families experiencing violence or unjust treatment because of their faith; teenage married couples; the elderly, who are often obliged to live alone with inadequate means of subsistence.

The *families of migrants*, especially in the case of manual workers and farm workers, should be able to find a homeland everywhere in the Church. This is a task stemming from the nature of the Church, as being the sign of unity in diversity. As far as possible these people should be looked after by priests of their own rite, culture, and language. It is also the Church's task to appeal to the public conscience and to all those in authority in social, economic, and political life, in order that workers may find employment in their own regions and homelands, that they may receive just wages, that their families may be reunited as soon as possible, be respected in their cultural identity and treated on an equal footing with others, and that their children may be given the chance to learn a trade and exercise it, as also the chance to own the land needed for working and living.

A difficult problem is that of the family which is *ideologically divided*. In these cases particular pastoral care is needed. In the first place it is necessary to maintain tactful personal contact with such families. The believing members must be strengthened in their faith and supported in their Christian lives. Although the party faithful to Catholicism cannot give way, dialogue with the other party must always be kept alive. Love and respect must be freely shown, in the firm hope that unity will be maintained. Much also depends on the relationship between parents and children. Moreover, ideologies which are alien to the faith can stimulate the believing members of the family to grow in faith and in the witness of love.

Other difficult circumstances in which the family needs the help of the ecclesial community and its pastors are: the children's adolescence, which can be disturbed, rebellious, and sometimes stormy; the children's marriage, which takes them away from their family; lack of understanding or lack of love on the part of those held most dear; abandonment by one of the spouses, or his or her death, which brings the painful experience of widowhood; or the death of a family member, which breaks up and deeply transforms the original family nucleus.

Similarly, the Church cannot ignore the time of old age, with all its positive and negative aspects. In old age married love, which has been increasingly purified and ennobled by long and unbroken fidelity, can be deepened. There is the opportunity of offering to others, in a new form, the kindness and the wisdom gathered over the years, and what energies remain. But there is also the burden of loneliness, more often psychological and emotional rather than physical, which results from abandonment or neglect on the part of children and relations. There is also suffering caused by ill-health, by the gradual loss of strength, by the humiliation of having to depend on others, by the sorrow of feeling that one is perhaps a burden to one's loved ones, and by the approach of the end of life. These are the circumstances in which, as the Synod Fathers suggested, it is easier to help people understand and live the lofty aspects of the spirituality of marriage and the family, aspects which take their inspiration from the value of Christ's cross and resurrection, the source of sanctification and profound happiness in daily life, in the light of the great eschatological realities of eternal life.

In all these different situations let prayer, the source of light and strength and the nourishment of Christian hope, never be neglected.

Mixed marriages

78. The growing number of mixed marriages between Catholics and other baptized persons also calls for special pastoral attention in the light of the directives and norms contained in the most recent documents of the Holy See and in those drawn up by the episcopal conferences, in order to permit their practical application to the various situations.

Couples living in a mixed marriage have special needs, which can be put under three main headings.

In the first place, attention must be paid to the obligations that faith imposes on the Catholic party with regard to the free exercise of the faith and the consequent obligation to ensure, as far as is possible, the baptism and upbringing of the children in the Catholic faith.[178]

There must be borne in mind the particular difficulties inherent in the relationships between husband and wife with regard to respect for religious freedom: this freedom could be violated either by undue pressure to make the partner change his or her beliefs or by placing obstacles in the way of the free manifestation of these beliefs by religious practice.

With regard to the liturgical and canonical form of marriage, Ordinaries can make wide use of their faculties to meet various necessities.

In dealing with these special needs, the following points should be kept in mind:

— In the appropriate preparation for this type of marriage, every reasonable effort must be made to ensure a proper understanding of Catholic teaching on the qualities and obligations of marriage, and also to ensure that the pressures and obstacles mentioned above will not occur.

— It is of the greatest importance that, through the support of the community, the Catholic party should be strengthened in faith and positively helped to mature in understanding and practicing that faith, so as to become a credible witness within the family through his or her own life and through the quality of love shown to the other spouse and the children.

Marriages between Catholics and other baptized persons have their own particular nature, but they contain numerous elements that could well be made good use of and developed, both for their intrinsic value and for the contribution that they can make to the ecumenical movement. This is particularly true when both parties are faithful to their religious duties. Their common baptism and the dynamism of grace provide the spouses in these marriages with the basis and motivation for expressing their unity in the sphere of moral and spiritual values.

For this purpose, and also in order to highlight the ecumenical importance of mixed marriages which are fully lived in the faith of the two Christian spouses, an effort should be made to establish cordial cooperation between the Catholic and the non-Catholic ministers from the time that preparations begin for the marriage and the wedding ceremony, even though this does not always prove easy.

With regard to the sharing of the non-Catholic party in Eucharistic Communion, the norms issued by the Secretariat for Promoting Christian Unity should be followed.[179]

Today in many parts of the world marriages between Catholics and non-baptized persons are growing in numbers. In many such marriages the non-baptized partner professes another religion, and his beliefs are to be treated with respect, in accordance with the principles set out in the Second Vatican Council's Declaration *Nostra Aetate* on relations with non-Christian religions. But in many other such marriages, particularly in secularized societies, the non-baptized person professes no religion at all. In these marriages there is a need for episcopal conferences and for individual bishops to ensure that there are proper pastoral safeguards for the faith of the Catholic partner and for the free exercise of his faith, above all in regard to his duty to do all in his power to ensure the Catholic baptism and education of the children of the marriage. Likewise the Catholic must be assisted in every possible way to offer within his family a genuine witness to the Catholic faith and to Catholic life.

Pastoral action in certain irregular situations

79. In its solicitude to protect the family in all its dimensions, not only the religious one, the Synod of Bishops did not fail to take into careful consideration certain situations which are irregular in a religious sense and often in the civil sense

too. Such situations, as a result of today's rapid cultural changes, are unfortunately becoming widespread also among Catholics with no little damage to the very institution of the family and to society, of which the family constitutes the basic cell.

a) Trial marriages

80. A first example of an irregular situation is provided by what are called "trial marriages," which many people today would like to justify by attributing a certain value to them. But human reason leads one to see that they are unacceptable, by showing the unconvincing nature of carrying out an "experiment" with human beings, whose dignity demands that they should be always and solely the term of a self-giving love without limitations of time or of any other circumstance.

The Church, for her part, cannot admit such a kind of union, for further and original reasons which derive from faith. For, in the first place, the gift of the body in the sexual relationship is a real symbol of the giving of the whole person: such a giving, moreover, in the present state of things cannot take place with full truth without the concourse of the love of charity, given by Christ. In the second place, marriage between two baptized persons is a real symbol of the union of Christ and the Church, which is not a temporary or "trial" union but one which is eternally faithful. Therefore between two baptized persons there can exist only an indissoluble marriage.

Such a situation cannot usually be overcome unless the human person, from childhood, with the help of Christ's grace and without fear, has been trained to dominate concupiscence from the beginning and to establish relationships of genuine love with other people. This cannot be secured without a true education in genuine love and in the right use of sexuality, such as to introduce the human person in every aspect, and therefore the bodily aspect too, into the fullness of the mystery of Christ.

It will be very useful to investigate the causes of this phenomenon, including its psychological and sociological aspect, in order to find the proper remedy.

b) De facto free unions

81. This means unions without any publicly recognized institutional bond, either civil or religious. This phenomenon, which is becoming ever more frequent, cannot fail to concern pastors of souls, also because it may be based on widely varying factors, the consequences of which may perhaps be containable by suitable action.

Some people consider themselves almost forced into a free union by difficult economic, cultural, or religious situations, on the grounds that, if they contracted a regular marriage, they would be exposed to some form of harm, would lose economic advantages, would be discriminated against, etc. In other cases, however, one encounters people who scorn, rebel against, or reject society, the institution of the family, and the social and political order, or who are solely seeking pleasure. Then there are those who are driven to such situations by extreme ignorance or poverty, sometimes by a conditioning due to situations of real injustice, or by a certain psychological immaturity that makes them uncertain or afraid to enter into a stable and definitive union. In some countries, traditional customs presume that the true and proper marriage will take place only after a period of cohabitation and the birth of the first child.

Each of these elements presents the Church with arduous pastoral problems, by reason of the serious consequences deriving from them, both religious and moral (the loss of the religious sense of marriage seen in the light of the covenant of God with his people, deprivation of the grace of the sacrament, grave scandal), and also social consequences (the destruction of the concept of the family, the weakening of the sense of fidelity, also toward society, possible psychological damage to the children, the strengthening of selfishness).

The pastors and the ecclesial community should take care to become acquainted with such situations and their actual causes, case by case. They should make tactful and respectful contact with the couples concerned, and enlighten them patiently, correct them charitably, and show them the witness of Christian family life, in such a way as to smooth the path for them to regularize their situation. But above all there must be a campaign of prevention, by fostering the sense of fidelity in the whole moral and religious training of the young, instructing them concerning the conditions and structures that favor such fidelity, without which there is no true freedom; they must be helped to reach spiritual maturity and enabled to understand the rich human and supernatural reality of marriage as a sacrament.

The People of God should also make approaches to the public authorities, in order that the latter may resist these tendencies which divide society and are harmful to the dignity, security, and welfare of the citizens as individuals, and they must try to ensure that public opinion is not led to undervalue the institutional importance of marriage and the family. And since in many regions young people are unable to get married properly because of extreme poverty deriving from unjust or inadequate social and economic structures, society and the public authorities should favor legitimate marriage by means of a series of social and political actions which will guarantee a family wage by issuing directives ensuring housing fitting for family life and by creating opportunities for work and life.

c) Catholics in civil marriages

82. There are increasing cases of Catholics who for ideological or practical reasons, prefer to contract a merely civil marriage and who reject or at least defer religious marriage. Their situation cannot of course be likened to that of people simply living together without any bond at all, because in the present case there is at least a certain commitment to a properly defined and probably stable state of life, even though the possibility of a future divorce is often present in the minds of those entering a civil marriage. By seeking public recognition of their bond on the part of the State, such couples show that they are ready to accept not only its advantages but also its obligations. Nevertheless, not even this situation is acceptable to the Church.

The aim of pastoral action will be to make these people understand the need for consistency between their choice of life and the faith that they profess, and to try to do everything possible to induce them to regularize their situation in the light of Christian principles. While treating them with great charity and bringing them into the life of the respective communities, the pastors of the Church will regrettably not be able to admit them to the sacraments.

d) Separated or divorced persons who have not remarried

83. Various reasons can unfortunately lead to the often irreparable breakdown of valid marriages. These include mutual lack of understanding and the inability to enter into interpersonal relationships. Obviously, separation must be considered as a last resort, after all other reasonable attempts at reconciliation have proved vain.

Loneliness and other difficulties are often the lot of separated spouses, especially when they are the innocent parties. The ecclesial community must support such people more than ever. It must give them much respect, solidarity, understanding, and practical help, so that they can preserve their fidelity even in their difficult situation; and it must help them to cultivate the need to forgive which is inherent in Christian love, and to be ready perhaps to return to their former married life.

The situation is similar for people who have undergone divorce, but, being well aware that the valid marriage bond is indissoluble, refrain from becoming involved in a new union and devote themselves solely to carrying out their family duties and the responsibilities of Christian life. In such cases their example of fidelity and Christian consistency takes on particular value as a witness before the world and the Church.

Here it is even more necessary for the Church to offer continual love and assistance, without there being any obstacle to admission to the sacraments.

e) Divorced persons who have remarried

84. Daily experience unfortunately shows that people who have obtained a divorce usually intend to enter into a new union, obviously not with a Catholic religious ceremony. Since this is an evil that, like the others, is affecting more and more Catholics as well, the problem must be faced with resolution and without delay. The Synod Fathers studied it expressly. The Church, which was set up to lead to salvation all people and especially the baptized, cannot abandon to their own devices those who have been previously bound by sacramental marriage and who have attempted a second marriage. The Church will therefore make untiring efforts to put at their disposal her means of salvation.

Pastors must know that, for the sake of truth, they are obliged to exercise careful discernment of situations. There is in fact a difference between those who have sincerely tried to save their first marriage and have been unjustly abandoned, and those who through their own grave fault have destroyed a canonically valid marriage. Finally, there are those who have entered into a second union for the sake of the children's upbringing, and who are sometimes subjectively certain in conscience that their previous and irreparably destroyed marriage had never been valid.

Together with the Synod, I earnestly call upon pastors and the whole community of the faithful to help the divorced, and with solicitous care to make sure that they do not consider themselves as separated from the Church, for as baptized persons they can, and indeed must, share in her life. They should be encouraged to listen to the word of God, to attend the Sacrifice of the Mass, to persevere in prayer, to contribute to works of charity and to community efforts in favor of justice, to bring up their children in the Christian faith, to cultivate the spirit and practice of penance and thus implore, day by day, God's grace. Let the Church pray for them, encourage them, and show herself a merciful mother, and thus sustain them in faith and hope.

However, the Church reaffirms her practice, which is based upon Sacred Scripture, of not admitting to Eucharistic Communion divorced persons who have remarried. They are unable to be admitted thereto from the fact that their state and condition of life objectively contradict that union of love between Christ and the Church which is signified and effected by the Eucharist. Besides this, there is another special pastoral reason: if these people were admitted to the Eucharist, the faithful would be led into error and confusion regarding the Church's teaching about the indissolubility of marriage.

Reconciliation in the sacrament of Penance, which would open the way to the Eucharist, can only be granted to those who, repenting of having broken the sign of the covenant and of fidelity to Christ, are sincerely ready to undertake a way of life that is no longer in contradiction to the indissolubility of marriage. This means, in practice, that when, for serious reasons, such as for example the children's upbringing, a man and a woman cannot satisfy the obligation to separate, they "take on themselves the duty to live in complete continence, that is, by abstinence from the acts proper to married couples."[180]

Similarly, the respect due to the sacrament of Matrimony, to the couples themselves and their families, and also to the community of the faithful, forbids any pastor, for whatever reason or pretext even of a pastoral nature, to perform ceremonies of any kind for divorced people who remarry. Such ceremonies would give the impression of the celebration of a new sacramentally valid marriage, and would thus lead people into error concerning the indissolubility of a validly contracted marriage.

By acting in this way, the Church professes her own fidelity to Christ and to his truth. At the same time she shows motherly concern for these children of hers, especially those who, through no fault of their own, have been abandoned by their legitimate partner.

With firm confidence she believes that those who have rejected the Lord's command and are still living in this state will be able to obtain from God the grace of conversion and salvation, provided that they have persevered in prayer, penance, and charity.

Those without a family

85. I wish to add a further word for a category of people whom, as a result of the actual circumstances in which they are living, and this often not through their own deliberate wish, I consider particularly close to the Heart of Christ and deserving of the affection and active solicitude of the Church and of pastors.

There exist in the world countless people who unfortunately cannot in any sense claim membership of what could be called in the proper sense a family. Large sections of humanity live in conditions of extreme poverty, in which promiscuity, lack of housing, the irregular nature and instability of relationships, and the extreme lack of education make it impossible in practice to speak of a true family. There are others who, for various reasons, have been left alone in the world. And yet for all of these people there exists a "good news of the family."

On behalf of those living in extreme poverty, I have already spoken of the urgent need to work courageously in order to find solutions, also at the political level, which will make it possible to help them and to overcome this inhuman condition of degradation.

It is a task that faces the whole of society but in a special way the authorities, by reason of their position and the responsibilities flowing therefrom, and also families, which must show great understanding and willingness to help.

For those who have no natural family the doors of the great family which is the Church—the Church which finds concrete expression in the diocesan and the parish family, in ecclesial basic communities, and in movements of the apostolate—must be opened even wider. No one is without a family in this world: the Church is a home and family for everyone, especially those who "labor and are heavy laden."[181]

Ponder

To introduce this section on families in difficult circumstances, Saint John Paul II evokes the Gospel image of Jesus as the Good Shepherd. Like Jesus, the Church and its pastors have a responsibility to seek out the straying, rejoice at their return (see Mt 18:12–14), and minister to the wounded. Pastors must also defend those in their care from predators, even to the point of laying down their lives (see Jn 10:18). Who are these families in difficulty? The Holy Father mentions a great range of situations: families of migrants or other itinerant persons, displaced or homeless families, families of those suffering from addiction, families experiencing persecution, families in poverty, families headed by single parents or teens, families divided by ideology, families challenged by dealing with adolescents or caring for the elderly, and those without families. But families of those in irregular marriage situations receive the most attention in this document.

Of particular concern are "trial marriages" (when people enter into a marriage-like state for a limited time), and "de facto free unions," which are indefinite in length (sometimes called "common law marriages"). In many countries the lines between these practices are blurred by the increasingly common practice of cohabitation. Pope John Paul II notes why the Church opposes these practices. They are contrary to reason and the good of persons. They fail to recognize that to give one's body in sexual intercourse is to give oneself and it is only the unconditional promise of the marriage covenant that makes this union a truthful expression of the relationship. We also now know, through decades of social scientific study, that those who live together before marriage are far more likely to have their marriages end in divorce.[*]

Divorce is a tragedy that affects many people in our world today and causes great suffering for men, women, and children. Sadly, it also affects many within the Church. Though both parties may bear some responsibility for the failure of the marriage, divorce itself does not bar a person from participating in the Church's sacramental life. Only those who have divorced and then civilly remarried outside of the Church cannot receive the sacraments. Why? Because civil divorce does not undo the bond of a sacramental marriage, so those in a second marriage live in a state that contradicts the fidelity they promised in their first marriage. There are three exceptions to this in the Church's practice. First, those who have divorced and civilly remarried may receive the sacraments if they receive an annulment and have their civil marriage convalidated (or "blessed") by the Church. (An annulment is generally a declaration by a Church tribunal that there was not a valid sacramental marriage in the first case). Second, couples in second marriages can be readmitted to the

---

[*] See the data and helpful pastoral advice in the USCCB study "Marriage Preparation and Cohabiting Couples," available at http://www.usccb.org/issues-and-action/marriage-and-family/marriage/marriage-preparation/cohabiting.cfm (accessed 9/26/14).

sacraments if they agree to live "as brother and sister" (i.e., in a non-sexual relationship). And third, individuals can receive the sacraments if they are in danger of death and have sincere contrition.

Those who have divorced and are in civil second marriages are not separated from the Church and should be encouraged "to listen to the word of God, to attend the Sacrifice of the Mass, to persevere in prayer, to contribute to works of charity and to community efforts in favor of justice, to bring up their children in the Christian faith, to cultivate the spirit and practice of penance and thus implore, day by day, God's grace" (*FC* no. 84). This often painful inability to fully participate in the Church's life calls for particular care of the divorced and remarried on the part of pastors and the whole Christian community.

1. One of the primary meanings of the word "pastor" is "shepherd," a term given to presbyters and bishops in the New Testament (see Acts 20:28; 1 Pt 5:1ff.). In your understanding, what does it mean for the Church's pastors to act as "shepherds" in their ministry to families?

2. In an interview given in the first year of his pontificate Pope Francis said: "the thing the Church needs most today is the ability to heal wounds and to warm the hearts of the faithful; it needs nearness, proximity. I see the Church as a field hospital after battle. It is useless to ask a seriously injured person if he has high cholesterol and about the level of his blood sugars! You have

to heal his wounds. Then we can talk about everything else. Heal the wounds, heal the wounds."* What are some of the most common wounds you see in the families around you? What wounds do you see in your own family? How might these wounds be healed?

3. Reflecting on the situation of divorced and remarried persons Pope Benedict XVI said: "I see here a great task for a parish, a Catholic community, to do whatever is possible to help them to feel loved and accepted, to feel that they are not 'excluded. . . .' They need to realize that this suffering is not just a physical or psychological pain, but something that is experienced within the Church community for the sake of the great values of our faith. I am convinced that their suffering, if truly accepted from within, is a gift to the Church. They need to know this, to realize that this is their way of serving the Church, that they are in the heart of the Church."† What can you do to make this a reality in your parish?

---

* See "A Big Heart Open to God," available at http://americamagazine.org/pope-interview (accessed 3/10/2014).

† Benedict XVI, "Evening of Witness: Address of His Holiness Pope Benedict XVI," Bresso Park, Milan, 2 June 2012, available at: http://www.vatican.va/holy_father/benedict_xvi/speeches/2012/june/documents/hf_ben-xvi_spe_20120602_festa-testimonianze_en.html (accessed 3/10/14).

Pray

Prayerfully read Jesus' words about himself as gatekeeper, gate, and shepherd of his sheep (Jn 10:1–18). Spend time praying that the bishops and priests of the Church might act as true shepherds to their flocks, especially to those who are suffering.

Act

Make an effort to reach out to a family or a person in your parish community whom you know is going through a difficult time. Tell them you are praying for them and ask how you could assist them.

Conclusion

86. At the end of this Apostolic Exhortation my thoughts turn with earnest solicitude:

— to you, married couples, to you, fathers and mothers of families;

— to you, young men and women, the future and the hope of the Church and the world, destined to be the dynamic central nucleus of the family in the approaching third millennium;

— to you, venerable and dear brothers in the episcopate and in the priesthood, beloved sons and daughters in the religious life, souls consecrated to the Lord, who bear witness before married couples to the ultimate reality of the love of God;

— to you, upright men and women, who for any reason whatever give thought to the fate of the family.

The future of humanity passes by way of the family.

It is therefore indispensable and urgent that every person of good will should endeavor to save and foster the values and requirements of the family.

I feel that I must ask for a particular effort in this field from the sons and daughters of the Church. Faith gives them full knowledge of God's wonderful plan: they therefore have an extra reason for caring for the reality that is the family in this time of trial and of grace.

They must show the family special love. This is an injunction that calls for concrete action.

Loving the family means being able to appreciate its values and capabilities, fostering them always. Loving the family means identifying the dangers and the evils that menace it, in order to overcome them. Loving the family means endeavoring to create for it an environment favorable for its development. The modern Christian family is often tempted to be discouraged and is distressed at the growth of its difficulties; it is an eminent form of love to give it back its reasons for confidence in itself, in the riches that it possesses by nature and grace, and in the mission that God has entrusted to it. "Yes indeed, the families of today must be called back to their original position. They must follow Christ."[182]

Christians also have the mission of proclaiming with joy and conviction the Good News about the family, for the family absolutely needs to hear ever anew and to understand ever more deeply the authentic words that reveal its identity, its inner resources, and the importance of its mission in the City of God and in that of man.

The Church knows the path by which the family can reach the heart of the deepest truth about itself. The Church has learned this path at the school of Christ and the school of history interpreted in the light of the Spirit. She does not impose it, but she feels an urgent need to propose it to everyone without fear and indeed with great confidence and hope, although she knows that the Good News includes the subject of the cross. But it is through the cross that the family can attain the fullness of its being and the perfection of its love.

Finally, I wish to call on all Christians to collaborate cordially and courageously with all people of good will who are serving the family in accordance with their responsibilities. The individuals and groups, movements, and associations in the Church which devote themselves to the family's welfare, acting in the Church's name and under her inspiration, often find themselves side by side with other individuals and institutions working for the same ideal. With faithfulness to the values of the Gospel and of the human person and with respect for lawful pluralism in initiatives, this collaboration can favor a more rapid and integral advancement of the family.

And now, at the end of my pastoral message, which is intended to draw everyone's attention to the demanding yet fascinating roles of the Christian family, I wish to invoke the protection of the Holy Family of Nazareth.

Through God's mysterious design, it was in that family that the Son of God spent long years of a hidden life. It is therefore the prototype and example for all Christian families. It was unique in the world. Its life was passed in anonymity and silence in a little town in Palestine. It underwent trials of poverty, persecution, and exile. It glorified God in an incomparably exalted and pure way. And it will not fail to help Christian families—indeed, all the families in the world—to be faithful to their day-to-day duties, to bear the cares and tribulations of life, to be open and generous to the needs of others, and to fulfill with joy the plan of God in their regard.

Saint Joseph was "a just man," a tireless worker, the upright guardian of those entrusted to his care. May he always guard, protect, and enlighten families.

May the Virgin Mary, who is the Mother of the Church, also be the Mother of "the church of the home." Thanks to her motherly aid, may each Christian family really become a "little church" in which the mystery of the Church of Christ is mirrored and given new life. May she, the Handmaid of the Lord, be an example of humble and generous acceptance of the will of God. May she, the Sorrowful Mother at the foot of the cross, comfort the sufferings and dry the tears of those in distress because of the difficulties of their families.

May Christ the Lord, the Universal King, the King of Families, be present in every Christian home as he was at Cana, bestowing light, joy, serenity, and strength. On the solemn day dedicated to his Kingship, I beg of him that every family may generously make its own contribution to the coming of his Kingdom in the world—"a kingdom of truth and life, a kingdom of holiness and grace, a kingdom of justice, love, and peace,"[183] toward which history is journeying.

I entrust each family to him, to Mary, and to Joseph. To their hands and their hearts I offer this Exhortation: may it be they who present it to you, venerable brothers and beloved sons and daughters, and may it be they who open your hearts to the light that the Gospel sheds on every family.

I assure you all of my constant prayers and I cordially impart the apostolic blessing to each and every one of you, in the name of the Father, and of the Son, and of the Holy Spirit.

Given in Rome, at Saint Peter's, on the twenty-second day of November, the Solemnity of our Lord Jesus Christ, Universal King, in the year 1981, the fourth of my pontificate.

Joannes Paulus pp. II

PONDER

At the end of this document the Pope of the family speaks to his audience from his heart. In addressing married couples, the young, and "all upright men and women" of the world, he calls them to love and work for the good of the family. He summons Christians to undertake the task of *"proclaiming with joy and conviction the Good News about the family"* (*FC* no. 86). Why? Because *"[t]he future of humanity passes by way of the family"* (*FC* no. 86). This truth, evident to our reason, is further illumined by biblical revelation.

Saint John Paul II closes by inviting his readers to reflect on the Holy Family of Nazareth—not because they lived an idyllic existence as some popular piety and art would have us imagine. In reality this family lived in anonymity and silence in an obscure little town. This family knew the trials of homelessness, persecution, exile, and poverty. In the midst of these challenges "it glorified God in an incomparably exalted and pure way" (*FC* no. 86). Christian families can find in the Holy Family's example, intercession, and protection the help that they need in the midst of their trials "to fulfill with joy the plan of God in their regard" (*FC* no. 86). He entrusts the families of the world into the hands of Joseph, Mary, and Jesus. We can follow his example and do the same with our families and those of the world today.

1. Do you understand the Church's teaching on marriage and family as part of the "good news"? What is your role in proclaiming "the gospel of the family"?

2. Think about why the future of humanity passes by the way of the family, and try to articulate this in your own words.

PRAY

In December 2013 Pope Francis invited the Church to pray with him for the coming Consistory and Synods on the Family, with the following prayer to the Holy Family. Pray it slowly now for the families of the Church and the world:

Jesus, Mary, and Joseph
in you we contemplate
the splendor of true love
to you we turn with trust.
Holy Family of Nazareth,
grant that our families too
may be places of communion and prayer,
authentic schools of the Gospel
and small domestic Churches.
Holy Family of Nazareth,
may families never again
experience violence, rejection, and division:
may all who have been hurt or scandalized
find ready comfort and healing.

Holy Family of Nazareth,
may the [. . .] Synod of Bishops
make us once more mindful
of the sacredness and inviolability of the family,
and its beauty in God's plan.
Jesus, Mary, and Joseph,
graciously hear our prayer.

Act

Commit yourself to pray for marriage and families on a regular basis. Ask Saint John Paul II to pray with you for this intention.

Notes

1. Cf. Second Vatican Ecumenical Council, *Gaudium et Spes*, 52.

2. Cf. John Paul II, Homily for the Opening of the Sixth Synod of Bishops (Sept. 26, 1980), 2: *AAS* 72 (1980), 1008.

3. Cf. Gn 1–2.

4. Cf. Eph 5.

5. Cf. *Gaudium et Spes*, 47; Pope John Paul II, Letter *Appropinquat Iam* (Aug. 15, 1980), 1: *AAS* 72 (1980), 791.

6. Cf. Mt 19:4.

7. Cf. *Gaudium et Spes*, 47.

8. Cf. John Paul II, Address to Council of the General Secretariat of the Synod of Bishops (Feb. 23, 1980): *Insegnamenti di Giovanni Paolo II*) III, I (1980), 472–476.

9. Cf. *Gaudium et Spes*, 4.

10. Cf. Second Vatican Ecumenical Council, *Lumen Gentium*, 12.

11. Cf. 1 Jn 2:20.

12. *Lumen Gentium*, 35.

13. Cf. *Lumen Gentium*, 12; Congregation for the Doctrine of the Faith, Declaration *Mysterium Ecclesiae*, 2: *AAS* 65 (1973), 398–400.

14. Cf. *Lumen Gentium*, 12; Second Vatican Ecumenical Council, Dogmatic Constitution on Divine Revelation *Dei Verbum*, 10.

15. Cf. John Paul II, Homily for the Opening of the Sixth Synod of Bishops, 3.

16. Cf. Saint Augustine, *De Civitate Dei*, XIV, 28; *CSEL* 40, II, 56–57.

17. *Gaudium et Spes*, 15.

18. Cf. Eph 3:8; *Gaudium et Spes*, 44; Second Vatican Ecumenical Council, Decree on the Missionary Activity of the Church *Ad Gentes*, 15, 22.

19. Cf. Mt 19:4–6.

20. Cf. Gn 1:26–27.

21. 1 Jn 4:8.

22. Cf. *Gaudium et Spes*, 12.

23. Cf. ibid., 48.

24. Cf. e.g., Hos 2:21; Jer 3:6–13; Is 54.

25. Ez 16:25.

26. Cf. Hos 3.

27. Cf. Gn 2:24; Mt 19:5.

28. Cf. Eph 5:32–33.

29. Tertullian, *Ad Uxorem*, II, VIII, 6–8: *CCL*, I, 393.

30. Cf. Council of Trent, Session XXIV, Canon 1: I. D. Mansi, *Sacrorum Conciliorum Nova et Amplissima Collectio*, 33, 149–150.

31. Cf. *Gaudium et Spes*, 48.

32. John Paul II, Address to the delegates of the Centre de Liaison des Equipes de Recherche (Nov. 3, 1979), 3: *Insegnamenti di Giovanni Paolo II*, 2 (1979), 1038.

33. Ibid., 4; loc. cit., 1032, 34. Cf. *Gaudium et Spes*, 50.

34. Cf. *Gaudium et Spes*, 50.

35. Cf. Gn 2:24.

36. Eph 3:15.

37. Cf. *Gaudium et Spes*, 78.

38. Saint John Chrysostom, *Virginity*, X: *PG* 48:540.

39. Cf. Mt 22:30.

40. Cf. 1 Cor 7:32–35.

41. Second Vatican Ecumenical Council, Decree on the Renewal of the Religious Life *Perfectae Caritatis*, 12.

42. Cf. Pius XII, Encyclical *Sacra Virginitas*, II: *AAS* 46 (1954), 174ff.

43. Cf. John Paul II, Letter *Novo Incipiente* (April 8, 1979), 9: *AAS* 71 (1979), 410–411.

44. *Gaudium et Spes*, 48.

45. John Paul II, Encyclical *Redemptor Hominis*, 10: *AAS* 71 (1979), 274.

46. Mt 19:6; cf. Gn 2:24.

47. Cf. John Paul II, Address to Married People at Kinshasa (May 3, 1980) 4: *AAS* 72 (1980), 426–427.

48. *Gaudium et Spes*, 49; cf. John Paul II, Address at Kinshasa 4: loc. cit.

49. *Gaudium et Spes*, 48.

50. Cf. Eph 5:25.

51. Mt 19:8.

52. Rev 3:14.

53. Cf. 2 Cor 1:20.

54. Cf. Jn 13:1.

55. Mt 19:6.

56. Rom 8:29.

57. Saint Thomas Aquinas, *Summa Theologiae*, II–II, q. 14, art. 2, ad 4.

58. *Lumen Gentium*, 11; cf. Second Vatican Ecumenical Council, Decree on the Apostolate of the Laity *Apostolicam Actuositatem*, 11.

59. *Gaudium et Spes*, 52.

60. Cf. Eph 6:1–4; Col 3:20–21.

61. Cf. *Gaudium et Spes*, 48.

62. Jn 17:21.

63. Cf. *Gaudium et Spes*, 24.

64. Gn 1:27.

65. Gal 3:26, 28.

66. Cf. John Paul II, Encyclical *Laborem Exercens*, 19: *AAS* 73 (1981), 625.

67. Gn 2:18.

68. Gn 2:23.

69. Saint Ambrose, *Exameron*, V 7, 19: *CSEL* 32, I, 154.

70. Paul VI, Encyclical *Humanae Vitae*, 9: *AAS* 60 (1968), 486.

71. Cf. Eph 5:25.

72. Cf. John Paul II, Homily to the Faithful of Terni (March 19, 1981), 3–5: *AAS* 73 (1981), 268–271.

73. Cf. Eph 3:15.

74. Cf. *Gaudium et Spes*, 52.

75. Lk 18:16; cf. Mt 19:14; Mk 18:16.

76. John Paul II, Address to the General Assembly of the United Nations (Oct. 2, 1979), 21: *AAS* 71 (1979), 1159.

77. Lk 2:52.

78. Cf. *Gaudium et Spes*, 48.

79. John Paul II, Address to the Participants in the International Forum on Active Aging (Sept. 5, 1980), 5: *Insegnamenti di Giovanni Paolo II*, III, 2 (1980), 539.

80. Gn 1:28.

81. Cf. Gn 5:1–3.

82. *Gaudium et Spes*, 50.

83. *Propositio* 21. Section 11 of the Encyclical *Humanae Vitae* ends with the statement: "The Church, calling people back to the observance of the norms of the natural law, as interpreted by her constant doctrine, teaches that each and every marriage act must remain open to the transmission of life *(ut quilibet matrimonii usus ad vitam humanam procreandam per se destinatus permaneat)*": *AAS* 60 (1968), 488.

84. Cf. 2 Cor 1:19; Rv 3:14.

85. Cf. the Sixth Synod of Bishops' Message to Christian Families in the Modern World (Oct. 24, 1980), 5.

86. *Gaudium et Spes*, 51.

87. *Humanae Vitae*, 7: *AAS* 60 (1968), 485.

88. Ibid., 12: loc. cit., 488–489.

89. Ibid., 14: loc. cit., 490.

90. Ibid., 13: loc. cit., 489.

91. Cf. *Gaudium et Spes*, 51.

92. *Humanae Vitae*, 29: *AAS* 60 (1968), 501.

93. Cf. Ibid., 25: loc. cit., 498–499.

94. Ibid., 21: loc. cit., 496.

95. John Paul II, Homily at the Close of the Sixth Synod of Bishops (Oct. 25, 1980), 8: *AAS* 72 (1980), 1083.

96. Cf. Paul VI, *Humanae Vitae*, 28: *AAS* 60 (1968), 501.

97. Cf. John Paul II, Address to the Delegates of the Centre de Liaison des Equipes de Recherche (Nov. 3, 1979), 9: *Insegnamenti di Giovanni Paolo II*, II, 2 (1979), 1035; and cf. Address to the Participants in the First Congress for the Family of Africa and Europe (Jan. 15, 1981): *L'Osservatore Romano*, Jan. 16, 1981.

98. *Humanae Vitae*, 25: *AAS* 60 (1968), 499.

99. Second Vatican Ecumenical Council, Declaration on Christian Education *Gravissimum Educationis*, 3.

100. *Gaudium et Spes*, 35.

101. Saint Thomas Aquinas, *Summa Contra Gentiles*, IV, 58.

102. *Gravissimum Educationis*, 2.

103. Paul VI, Apostolic Exhortation *Evangelii Nuntiandi*, 71: *AAS* 68 (1976), 60–61.

104. Cf. *Gravissimum Educationis*, 3.

105. *Apostolicam Actuositatem*, 11.

106. *Gaudium et Spes*, 52.

107. Cf. *Apostolicam Actuositatem*, 11.

108. Rom 12:13.

109. Mt 10:42.

110. Cf. *Gaudium et Spes*, 30.

111. Second Vatican Ecumenical Council, Declaration on Religious Freedom *Dignitatis Humanae*, 5.

112. Cf. *Propositio* 42.

113. *Lumen Gentium*, 31.

114. Cf. *Lumen Gentium*, 11; *Apostolicam Actuositatem*, 11; Pope John Paul II, Homily for the Opening of the Sixth Synod of Bishops (Sept. 26, 1980), 3: *AAS* 72 (1980), 1008.

115. *Lumen Gentium*, 11.

116. Cf. ibid., 41.

117. Acts 4:32.

118. Cf. *Humanae Vitae*, 9.

119. *Gaudium et Spes*, 48.

120. Cf. *Dei Verbum*, 1.

121. Rom 16:26.

122. Cf. *Humanae Vitae*, 25.

123. *Evangelii Nuntiandi*, 71.

124. Cf. Address to the Third General Assembly of the Bishops of Latin America (Jan. 28, 1979), IV a: *AAS* 71(1979), 204.

125. *Lumen Gentium*, 35.

126. John Paul II, Apostolic Exhortation *Catechesi Tradendae*, 68: *AAS* 71 (1979), 1334.

127. Cf. Ibid., 36: loc. cit., 1308

128. Cf. 1 Cor 12:4–6; Eph 4:12–13.

129. Mk 16:15.

130. Cf. *Lumen Gentium*, 11.

131. Acts 1:8.

132. Cf. 1 Pt 3:1–2.

133. *Lumen Gentium*, 35; cf. *Apostolicam Actuositatem*, 11.

134. Cf. Acts 18; Rom 16:3–4.

135. Cf. *Ad Gentes,* 39.

136. *Apostolicam Actuositatem*, 30.

137. Cf. *Lumen Gentium*, 10.

138. *Gaudium et Spes*, 49.

139. Ibid., 48.

140. Cf. *Lumen Gentium*, 41.

141. Second Vatican Ecumenical Council, Constitution on the Sacred Liturgy *Sacrosanctum Concilium*, 59.

142. Cf. 1 Pt 2:5; *Lumen Gentium*, 34.

143. *Lumen Gentium*, 34.

144. *Sacrosanctum Concilium*, 78.

145. Cf. Jn 19:34.

146. Section 25: *AAS* 60 (1968), 499.

147. Eph 2:4.

148. Cf. John Paul II, Encyclical *Dives in Misericordia*, 13: *AAS* 72 (1980), 1218–1219.

149. 1 Pt 2:5.

150. Mt 18:19–20.

151. *Gravissimum Educationis*, 3; cf. Pope John Paul II, *Catechesi Tradendae*, 36: *AAS* 71 (1979), 1308.

152. General Audience Address, Aug. 11, 1976: *Insegnamenti di Paolo VI*, XIV (1976), 640.

153. Cf. *Sacrosanctum Concilium*, 12.

154. Cf. *Institutio Generalis de Liturgia Horarum*, 27.

155. Paul VI, Apostolic Exhortation *Marialis Cultus*, 52, 54: *AAS* 66 (1974), 160–161.

156. John Paul II, Address at the Mentorella Shrine (Oct. 29, 1978): *Insegnamenti di Giovanni Paolo II*, I (1978), 78–79.

157. Cf. *Apostolicam Actuositatem*, 4.

158. Cf. John Paul I, Address to the Bishops of the 12th Pastoral Region of the United States (Sept. 21, 1978): *AAS*, 70 (1978), 767.

159. Rom 8:2.

160. Rom 5:5.

161. Cf. Mk 10:45.

162. *Lumen Gentium*, 36.

163. *Apostolicam Actuositatem*, 8.

164. Cf. the Sixth Synod of Bishops' Message to Christian Families (Oct. 24, 1980), 12.

165. Cf. John Paul II, Address to the Third General Assembly of the Bishops of Latin America (Jan. 28, 1979), IV a: *AAS* 71 (1979), 204.

166. Cf. *Sacrosanctum Concilium*, 10.

167. Cf. *Ordo Celebrandi Matrimonium*, 17.

168. Cf. *Sacrosanctum Concilium*, 59.

169. *Perfectae Caritatis*, 12.

170. John Paul II, Address to the Confederation of Family Advisory Bureaus of Christian Inspiration (Nov. 29, 1980), 3–4: *Insegnamenti di Giovanni Paolo II*, III, 2 (1980), 1453–1454.

171. Paul VI, Message for the Third Social Communications Day (April 7, 1969): *AAS* 61 (1969), 455.

172. John Paul II, Message for the 1980 World Social Communications Day (May 1, 1980): *Insegnamenti di Giovanni Paolo II*, III, 1 (1980), 1042.

173. John Paul II, Message for the 1981 World Social Communications Day (May 10, 1981), 5: *L'Osservatore Romano*, May 22, 1981.

174. Ibid.

175. Paul VI, Message for the Third Social Communications Day: *AAS* 61 (1969), 456.

176. Ibid.

177. John Paul II, Message for the 1980 World Social Communications Day, loc. cit., 1044.

178. Cf. Paul VI, Motu Proprio *Matrimonia Mixta*, 4–5: *AAS* 62 (1970), 257–259; John Paul II, Address to the Participants in the Plenary Meeting of the Secretariat for Promoting Christian Unity (Nov. 13, 1981): *L'Osservatore Romano*, Nov. 14, 1981.

179. Instruction *In Quibus Rerum Circumstantiis* (June 15, 1972): *AAS* 64 (1972), 518–525; Note of Oct. 17, 1973; *AAS* 65 (1973), 616–619.

180. John Paul II, Homily at the Close of the Sixth Synod of Bishops (Oct. 25, 1980), 7: *AAS* 72 (1980), 1082.

181. Mt 11:28.

182. John Paul II, Letter *Appropinquat Iam* (Aug. 15, 1980), 1: *AAS* 72 (1980), 791.

183. The Roman Missal, Preface of Christ the King.

 JOHN AND CLAIRE GRABOWSKI have been married for thirty years, have been blessed with five children, and are expecting their second grandchild. For over twenty years, the Grabowskis have been involved in marriage preparation and have given marriage talks and retreats as a couple. John has been on the faculty of the Catholic University of America in Washington, D.C., for twenty-four years. In September 2009, John and Claire were appointed by Pope Benedict XVI to serve as a member couple on the Pontifical Council for the Family. They also serve together in a "post-Cana" marriage ministry in their home parish of Saint Ignatius of Loyola in Ijamsville, Maryland.

BOOKS & MEDIA

A mission of the Daughters of St. Paul

As apostles of Jesus Christ, evangelizing today's world:

We are CALLED to holiness
by God's living Word and Eucharist.

We COMMUNICATE the Gospel message
through our lives and through all
available forms of media.

We SERVE the Church
by responding to the hopes and needs
of all people with the Word of God,
in the spirit of St. Paul.

For more information visit our website: www.pauline.org.

BOOKS & MEDIA

The Daughters of St. Paul operate book and media centers at the following addresses. Visit, call, or write the one nearest you today, or find us at www.pauline.org

CALIFORNIA

3908 Sepulveda Blvd, Culver City, CA 90230	310-397-8676
935 Brewster Avenue, Redwood City, CA 94063	650-369-4230
5945 Balboa Avenue, San Diego, CA 92111	858-565-9181

FLORIDA

145 S.W. 107th Avenue, Miami, FL 33174	305-559-6715

HAWAII

1143 Bishop Street, Honolulu, HI 96813	808-521-2731

ILLINOIS

172 North Michigan Avenue, Chicago, IL 60601	312-346-4228

LOUISIANA

4403 Veterans Memorial Blvd, Metairie, LA 70006	504-887-7631

MASSACHUSETTS

885 Providence Hwy, Dedham, MA 02026	781-326-5385

MISSOURI

9804 Watson Road, St. Louis, MO 63126	314-965-3512

NEW YORK

64 W. 38th Street, New York, NY 10018	212-754-1110

SOUTH CAROLINA

243 King Street, Charleston, SC 29401	843-577-0175

TEXAS

Currently no book center; for parish exhibits or outreach evangelization, contact: 210-569-0500, or SanAntonio@paulinemedia.com, or P.O. Box 761416, San Antonio, TX 78245

VIRGINIA

1025 King Street, Alexandria, VA 22314	703-549-3806

CANADA

3022 Dufferin Street, Toronto, ON M6B 3T5	416-781-9131

¡También somos su fuente para libros,
videos y música en español!